BUSINESS YOGA

Advance Praise for
Business Yoga

"Business, like yoga, is a path of discipline and purpose. It is not just about wealth creation but a duty—one that, when done with integrity, benefits society while fulfilling personal needs in moderation. Anil Kariwala's Business Yoga beautifully blends ancient wisdom with modern business principles, showing how mindful leadership can create not just success, but harmony and fulfillment. His insights offer a guiding light for those who seek to build businesses that are not only profitable but also purposeful and conscious."

~ *Sajjan Bhajanka, Padma Shri Awardee and Chairman, CenturyPly Group*

"Anil Kariwala has written a must-read compendium for anyone in business about how to facilitate energy awareness with conscious business for joyful and present enterprise. Weaving references to ancient yogic wisdom as well as business masters, contemporary authors, and practical ways to apply the knowledge, this text is replete with information presented in a thoughtful and insightful way. Read this book and absorb for a fresh, yet familiar, way of doing business successfully in every sense of the word."

~ *Lynn Scheurell, Business advisor, Author, and Transformation teacher*

"Anil Kariwala has brilliantly combined ancient yogic wisdom with modern business thinking in Business Yoga. By drawing on the seven chakras, he shows how businesses must cultivate balance, awareness, and resilience to succeed. This book blends insightful management concepts with real-world examples, offering both intellectual rigor and practical value. Whether you're a CEO or an entrepreneur, Business Yoga provides a transformative approach that moves beyond profit to purpose, from stress to flow, and from rigidity to alignment."

~ Darius Teter, Executive Director, Stanford Seed, Stanford Graduate School of Business

"A well-researched, insightful guide that connects ancient yoga wisdom to modern business best practices. With practical exercises and insights from top thought leaders, this book inspires mindful, ethical leadership for today's world."

~ Rick Levine, Executive Director, NAUMD

"Doing business is nothing more than expressing our values in a different context from our everyday lives. A context where personal values are tested even more because there is a concrete external factor that influences them: money, the most evident expression of the ego's affirmation. This is why this book holds value beyond just business. It conveys concepts that help us remain true to our everyday values, even in the business world. I have known Anil for over 15 years, both personally and professionally. His greatest strength is having stayed true to his deep personal values while bringing them into the world of business—something truly rare. I hope this book inspires a new generation of leaders like Anil. The world desperately needs them."

~ Matteo Borri, Kimood K-up, Kariban Brands

"Business Yoga delves deep into ancient Indian yogic philosophy to enunciate management principles for running modern day businesses. In doing so, it stresses harmony between business, its stakeholders, and the ecosystem just as the practice of yoga teaches us to strive for achieving harmony between the mind, body and our surroundings. Through his pursuit of these very practical principles, Anil does great service to millions of businesses - large and small - which will strengthen the culture of entrepreneurship."

~ Rahul Shukla, Group Head, HDFC Bank

"Business Yoga by Anil Kariwala comes as a solace when the business landscape across the world is pondering over VUCA, ESG etc. The book delights you dwelling upon the Seven Chakras and Eight limbs of yoga to business. It demystifies the complex business frameworks into orchestrated simple practice. It guides the business leaders to conduct business with a humane touch and is highly relevant in the world debating sustainability and circularity. A compelling read for all entrepreneurs and executives, the book offers excellent actionable insights to leaders to create organisations with human touch and deeper values. It's a testimony to ancient wisdom for today's business. I compliment the passion Anil poured in throughout Business Yoga like a Yogi..."

~ Dr.K.Rangarajan, Professor and Head, Indian Institute of Foreign Trade

"It has been a privilege to know Anil personally, and I believe he has put all his wisdom into this book, 'Business Yoga'. This thought-provoking work brings ancient yogic wisdom and business practices together, offering a unique perspective. The best part of this book is the way it blends philosophical concepts into business insights with clarity and a captivating style. 'Business Yoga' is a comprehensive resource for various business concepts, and I highly recommend it to all business professionals seeking a more balanced and purposeful approach to leadership with strong spiritual clarity."

~ Rajasekhar Parcha, CoFounder & CEO, GoApptiv

BUSINESS YOGA

ANCIENT WISDOM FOR MODERN BUSINESSES

ANIL KARIWALA

Copyright © Anil Kariwala 2025
All Rights Reserved.

ISBN
Paperback 979-8-89724-270-2
Hardcase 979-8-89744-648-3

This book has been published with all efforts taken to make the material error-free after the consent of the author. However, the author and the publisher do not assume and hereby disclaim any liability to any party for any loss, damage, or disruption caused by errors or omissions, whether such errors or omissions result from negligence, accident, or any other cause.

While every effort has been made to avoid any mistake or omission, this publication is being sold on the condition and understanding that neither the author nor the publishers or printers would be liable in any manner to any person by reason of any mistake or omission in this publication or for any action taken or omitted to be taken or advice rendered or accepted on the basis of this work. For any defect in printing or binding the publishers will be liable only to replace the defective copy by another copy of this work then available.

In loving memory of my father,

who risked everything to help

me embark on my journey

as an entrepreneur.

Contents

Foreword

The first meeting with Anil immediately felt like a gift. They say great minds think alike, and in our case, that is certainly true. The fun part is that we come from completely different backgrounds. I am a reformed boy from the cold Dutch soil, and Anil is from India with a completely different background. But upbringing and background do not matter when the values that drive you in life are the same. In our case, this was more than true. I only met Anil a few years ago. Our companies had been doing business for years, but our paths had never crossed. On a cold, gray spring day in the Netherlands, during a lunch, we finally got to know each other better. There was an immediate click, both personally and professionally.

I told Anil about my motivations and the values behind our company Dille & Kamille. Anil, in turn, shared how he wants Kariwala Industries to be more than just a company focused on short-term profits. Our conversations have not stopped since. I received all sorts of ideas and reflections from Anil about how he approaches business issues in a philosophical way.

I promised him I would visit India to have more extensive discussions with him. Our company strives to be a business for good. We want to give back more to the earth than we take from it. We want to be good to our customers, but also to our employees and suppliers. We jump through various hoops to obtain beautiful certificates such as B-Corp. We can do all this because our founder Freek Kamerling thought 50 years ago that a retail company could be much more than the products it sells. Anil, of course, knew our company as a supplier but was also touched by our founder's philosophy and the company that emerged from it. This allowed us to connect on a deeper spiritual level.

I kept my word, and in the fall of 2024, I visited Anil in Kolkata. During our trip, he enthusiastically talked about chakras and other yoga principles that he tried to apply in his business practices to promote balance, awareness, and sustainable growth. He also mentioned that he was writing a book titled Business Yoga. As a down-to-earth Dutchman, I had never really delved into yoga. Curiosity sparked by Anil's enthusiastic stories and clear examples; I did start to explore it a bit. The problem with us humans is that there is so much wisdom in the world, but we repeatedly manage to banish this ancient wisdom from our lives. Whether it concerns wisdom about our physical and mental health or how we interact with nature, we remain strange creatures who quickly forget or, worse, ignore all the good we have collectively gathered.

In his book Business Yoga, Anil shows how ancient yoga wisdom can contribute to balanced and conscious businesses. He explains how the principles of body, mind, and consciousness can be integrated into daily business operations. Each of the seven chakras is linked to important business aspects such as stability, creativity, leadership, empathy, communication, intuition, and purposefulness.

Thank you, Anil, for these valuable insights and for introducing me to the principles behind yoga. I am more than intrigued and have learned a tremendous amount. This confirms my belief that companies only have value if they are good for society, nature, and, above all, the people who work there. Hopefully, our companies will continue to collaborate for a long time.

Hans Geels
CEO, Dille & Kamille International, The Netherlands

Introduction: Business Yoga

Ancient Wisdom for Modern Businesses

Can the ancient wisdom of Yoga offer a path to balanced, conscious, and successful businesses?

Business is an integral part of life, driving innovation, progress, and economic growth. Its primary goal is to improve our *Standard of Living*. Yet, in the relentless pursuit of financial success, many organizations lose sight of deeper, more fulfilling goals.

Yoga, on the other hand, is centered around the *Standard of Life*—fostering trust, discipline, and fulfillment. Now, imagine applying these same principles to business, which, like a human being, has a body, mind, and consciousness. *Business Yoga* bridges this divide, offering Yoga as a philosophy that transforms how we approach work, leadership, and organizational culture.

The focus on growth and performance often overshadows the importance of balanced decision-making and thoughtful leadership. By incorporating harmony, mindfulness, and intentionality, *Business Yoga* redefines success—ensuring it is sustainable, meaningful, and enriching for all involved.

This holistic approach lies at the core of *Business Yoga*. By addressing both material and emotional dimensions of success, businesses can thrive economically while creating environments that nurture well-being and purpose for all.

Why I Began Writing This Book

The idea for this book began several years ago, when visitors to Kariwala Industries consistently commented on one remarkable aspect of our company: the palpable joy radiating from our employees. It was not something we had explicitly set out to achieve, yet it became one of our most defining characteristics. Time and again, I was asked, "How are your employees so happy? What is the secret?" These questions planted the seed for what became *Business Yoga*.

As an avid Yoga practitioner, I have long experienced the transformative power of its principles in my personal and professional life. *Business Yoga* is my attempt to share that journey, blending the ancient wisdom of Yoga with modern business practices. It offers a holistic approach to leadership, team building, and organizational success. While many associate Yoga with physical postures or personal well-being, its philosophy runs much deeper—encompassing timeless principles of discipline, balance, clarity, and purpose. These are as vital in the boardroom as they are on the yoga mat.

What This Book Offers

Many concepts discussed in this book are rooted in ancient Sanskrit, carrying profound depth that is often lost in translation. To make them accessible, they are presented in a simple and relatable manner, ensuring clarity for readers, regardless of their familiarity with philosophy or business.

Business Yoga guides readers through the intersection of Yoga's philosophy and modern business practices. It introduces concepts such as balance, awareness, and thoughtful leadership, addressing contemporary challenges. The chapters explore:

- The Seven Chakras (energy centers) and their parallels in organizational frameworks.
- The role of Ida and Pingala energy channels (intuition and logic) in decision-making.
- The application of Ashtanga Yoga's Eight Limbs to business principles, promoting balance within the Chakras.
- Strategies to enhance work-life integration, recognizing that work is an integral part of life, not separate from it.

A Valuable Resource for Further Learning

At the end of the book, you will find appendices that delve into concepts omitted earlier in the interest of brevity, along with a curated bibliography featuring concise synopses of each referenced work. This is more than a mere list of titles and authors—it distills the core ideas of these works into accessible insights. Additionally, many Yogic principles discussed throughout this book resonate with contemporary business thinkers who have reshaped global leadership and organizational practices.

An Invitation to Reflect

This book is not meant to be read in one sitting, nor does it offer quick fixes or success checklists. Instead, it encourages you to pause, reflect, and reconnect with what truly matters. Readers are invited to immerse themselves in the material, allowing its principles to resonate and inspire lasting, meaningful change.

As you journey through these pages, you will discover how ancient wisdom can guide modern businesses toward becoming not only profitable but also conscious, joyful, and purposeful. This is *Business Yoga*: a guide to balance, sustainability, and lasting impact.

PART ONE

The WHAT.

"It is not the strongest of the species that survive, nor the most intelligent, but the one most responsive to change."

— Charles Darwin

A Brief History of Business

When I was in high school, one concept left me both fascinated and perplexed: the concept of a business as a perpetual entity. We were taught that companies had the potential to outlast their founders, employees, and shareholders, legally structured to exist indefinitely. The idea that something as complex as a business could continue forever intrigued me. It also raised a paradox. In my physics class, the concept of perpetual motion—the idea of a machine that could run indefinitely on its own—was clearly debunked as impossible. So, if perpetual motion defies the laws of physics, how could a business be perpetual? Business seemed to mirror the impossibility of such a feat, yet some defied the odds, thriving across centuries while others crumbled within a few years. This apparent contradiction planted a seed of curiosity that has stayed with me ever since.

This confusion set me on a journey to understand the nature of business, its longevity, and the factors that enable some to endure across generations while others collapse within just a few years. I was reminded of ancient stories of Amrit -

the divine nectar that grants immortality, and the Chiranjeevis, the immortals of Hindu scriptures. In these stories, immortality is not just about physical survival; it requires continuous consciousness—an awareness that never wavers. Could it be that business, like the Chiranjeevis, requires a form of continuous consciousness to survive for centuries?

The Evolution of Business Structures

Historically, businesses evolved from small proprietorships to complex corporations. Early businesses dissolved with the death of their owners, lacking structures for continuity. The Dutch East India Company (VOC), founded in 1602, revolutionized this by creating a joint-stock company that allowed investors to pool resources and share risks. This innovation enabled businesses to transcend individual lifetimes, laying the foundation for modern corporations. It reflected the importance of principles of shared responsibility and collaboration.

The Industrial Revolution further transformed businesses into large-scale operations, employing thousands in factories. While this period marked significant progress, it also exposed the darker side of business—exploitation and unsafe working conditions. Iconic incidents like the Triangle Shirtwaist Factory fire in 1911 and the Rana Plaza collapse in 2013 highlighted the need for ethical practices and human-centered management. These events underscored the importance of balancing growth with human well-being.

Management Principles

As business grew in complexity, the separation of ownership and management became essential. Professional managers took over, enabling organizations to expand. This shift gave rise to formal business education, starting with the establishment of ESCP Europe in 1819 and later Harvard Business School in 1908. These institutions laid the groundwork for modern management, focusing on principles like efficiency, strategy, and leadership.

In the early 20th century, theorists like Frederick Winslow Taylor and Henri Fayol introduced scientific and administrative management principles. Taylor's *The Principles of Scientific Management* emphasized efficiency through task optimization, while Fayol's *General and Industrial Management* focused on planning, organizing, leading, and controlling. Max Weber's bureaucracy model further formalized organizational structures. While these approaches brought discipline to business operations, they often overlooked the human element, which became a focus of later theories.

The Human Relations Movement, led by Elton Mayo in the 1920s, shifted focus to employee well-being. Mayo's Hawthorne Studies revealed that workers are motivated by social factors and recognition, not just monetary rewards. This marked the beginning of more holistic management theories, which Peter Drucker later advanced. Drucker's *Management by Objectives* emphasized balancing individual goals with organizational objectives, emphasizing the importance of aligning individual effort with collective goals.

Business Gurus

The Sanskrit word "Guru" combines "Gu" (darkness) and "Ru" (remover), symbolizing a dispeller of ignorance. In the late 20th century, management gurus like Michael Porter and Gary Hamel introduced frameworks for strategic thinking and innovation. Porter's *Competitive Strategy* and the *Five Forces Model* remain cornerstones for analyzing industry competition. Meanwhile, Hamel's *The Future of Management* highlighted the need to empower employees and foster creativity—a concept centered on empowering individuals while fostering collaboration.

Despite these advancements, many businesses faltered due to their inability to adapt to change. Kodak, Blockbuster, and Nokia are cautionary tales of companies that failed to evolve with technological and market shifts. In contrast, businesses like Saint-Gobain and Kongo Gumi demonstrate the power of adaptability and resilience. Saint-Gobain, founded in 1665, transitioned from glass manufacturing to high-performance materials over centuries. Kongo Gumi, a Japanese construction company established in 578 AD, thrived for over 1,400 years by balancing tradition and innovation.

These stories demonstrate the importance of continuous self-awareness and adaptability, highlighting how businesses must stay attuned to changing environments to thrive.

Compulsive and Conscious Business

In examining the history of business, it becomes evident that they fall into two categories: compulsive and conscious. Compulsive businesses operate reactively, driven by immediate pressures and short-term gains. They often lack a clear sense of purpose, leading to burnout and eventual failure. Conscious businesses, on the other hand, balance profitability with ethical practices and long-term vision. Movements like Conscious Capitalism, championed by John Mackey and Raj Sisodia, exemplify this approach. Their book, *Conscious Capitalism: Liberating the Heroic Spirit of Business*, argues that companies should integrate social responsibility, environmental sustainability, and stakeholder well-being into their models.

Similarly, thought leaders like Simon Sinek and Brene Brown have reshaped leadership paradigms. Sinek's *Start with Why* encourages businesses to operate with a clear sense of purpose, inspiring trust and loyalty. Brown's *Dare to Lead* underscores the importance of vulnerability and authenticity in leadership. These ideas emphasize self-awareness and intentional action—leading with purpose and compassion.

Frederic Laloux's *Reinventing Organizations* introduces self-management and evolutionary purpose as pillars of modern business. Teal Organizations prioritize adaptability and decentralized decision-making, highlighting harmony and balance in their operations. Companies like Patagonia and Buurtzorg exemplify these values, operating with conscious missions and empowering their teams. This evolution of decision-making showcases how shifts toward intentional strategies have contributed to sustainability and long-term success.

Sustainability and Ethical Practices

The emergence of Certified B Corporations illustrates ethical and sustainable practices. These businesses meet rigorous social and environmental standards, proving that profit and purpose can coexist. Similarly, Sedex-audited businesses, which ensure responsible supply chains, represent another vital approach to sustainability. These efforts highlight the importance of ethical responsibility and sustainable business practices in addressing modern challenges.

As businesses evolved in tandem with growing environmental and social challenges, additional frameworks such as the Triple Bottom Line emerged, advocating for a balance between profit, people, and the planet. John Elkington, who coined this term, highlighted the need for businesses to measure their success not just in financial terms but also through their environmental and social impact. These concepts underscore the interconnectedness between actions and their ripple effects.

Expanding Awareness

To understand how businesses approached awareness in history, we can look at examples such as Tata Group, which was ahead of its time in prioritizing employee welfare in the

20th century. By introducing pension funds and insurance for employees, they exemplified a forward-thinking approach rooted in care and responsibility. Similarly, businesses that implement proactive measures for environmental sustainability—such as Unilever's Sustainable Living Plan— demonstrate an evolved sense of corporate mindfulness. These historical examples demonstrate the importance of foresight and ethical responsibility.

Awareness is not only about strategy but also about embracing humanity. Historical management thinkers like Mary Parker Follett (often regarded as the "Mother of Modern Management") championed the human side of organizations, advocating for community-centric approaches. Her ideas set the foundation for recognizing the emotional and social aspects of leadership that remain crucial today. The historical trajectory of business, when viewed through the lens of awareness, reveals that sustainable success requires organizations to be consistently conscious of their internal and external ecosystems.

A Conscious Path Forward

The history of business reveals a recurring theme: survival requires more than structural innovations. It demands a conscious connection to purpose and the ability to adapt. By embracing ancient principles of awareness, balance, and intentionality, businesses can transform into resilient, purpose-driven entities that not only survive but thrive in harmony with their surroundings.

The journey of business reflects the balancing of internal strength with external action. To thrive, businesses must integrate purpose, people, and process, creating a sustainable framework for long-term success. This blend of historical lessons and forward-thinking strategies offers a blueprint for businesses aiming to create lasting value. To truly understand how businesses can thrive in today's dynamic world, we must delve into ancient principles that offer timeless wisdom for achieving balance and sustainable growth.

Yoga: Body, Mind and Consciousness

Yoga, like many Sanskrit terms, defies exact translation into any other language. Its meanings encompass "union," "to yoke," "adding," and "harmonizing." In the West, Yoga is often perceived as a physical fitness routine aimed at strengthening the body and sharpening the mind. However, Yoga's essence runs much deeper—it's an ancient science that harmonizes the body, mind, and consciousness.

Every human pursuit has two purposes: to enhance the standard of living—providing material comfort and convenience—and to elevate the standard of life, cultivating inner peace and fulfillment. While modern society often prioritizes the former, it is only with the latter that true balance and meaning emerge. At the same time, material pursuits greatly enhance and make it easier to raise the standard of life.

In any field—business, arts, or science—the ultimate aim is to elevate the human experience. Yoga syncs perfectly with this mission, as it enriches the standard of life by fostering balance within our body, mind, and consciousness.

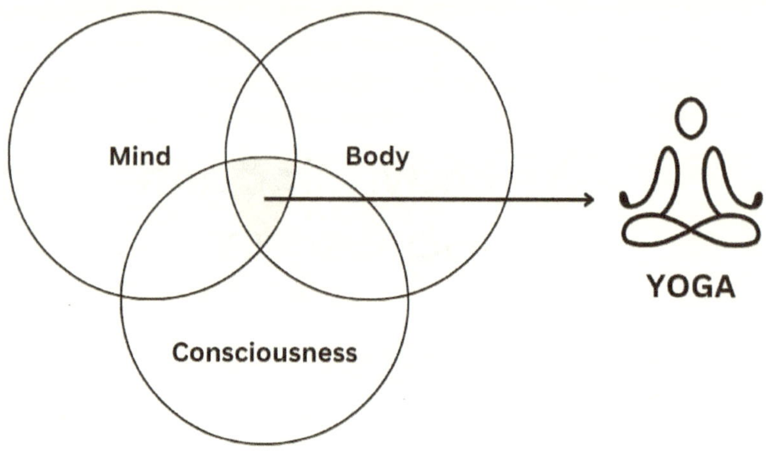

Yoga's roots stretch back thousands of years to Indian culture, with its philosophical foundation found in the *Yoga Sutras of Patanjali*. These 196 sutras, compiled in the 2nd century BCE, encapsulate timeless wisdom. At its core, Yoga aims to bring harmony to our inner and outer lives by uniting our body, mind, and consciousness.

As an amateur musician, I have experienced firsthand the importance of harmony. Just as in music, where individual talent means little without synchronization, our bodies and minds must be in perfect harmony to function at their best. A musician's timing is guided by the metronome—a consistent beat that ensures every note is perfectly placed. Yoga serves a similar purpose in life, acting as a metronome for our physical and mental well-being. Without harmony, we become dissonant, much like a performance where each musician plays at their own tempo.

Yoga achieves harmony in two key ways:

1. **Balancing the Seven Chakras**: These energy centers, located along the spine, influence our physical, emotional, and spiritual health. Achieving balance between them brings a sense of flow and well-being.

2. **Harmonizing the Ida and Pingala Energy Channels**: These two channels run along the spine, representing the dual forces within us—masculine and feminine, logic and intuition. Keeping them in balance is crucial for our overall energy flow and health.

Yoga provides this harmony through Ashtanga Yoga, which is based on eight limbs, each offering a path to physical, mental, and spiritual well-being. Just like a metronome guides musicians, the principles of Yoga guide us toward a more balanced and fulfilling life.

PART TWO

The WHY.

"He who has a why to live can bear almost any how."

— Friedrich Nietzsche

The Seven Chakras

Chakras serve as the vital link between the mind and the body, acting as energy centers that regulate the flow of Prana, or life energy, within us. Derived from the Sanskrit word for "wheel," a chakra represents a spinning vortex of energy, where the various energy channels, or Nadis, intersect. Imagine chakras as dynamic hubs—similar to railway junctions or airport hubs— where different routes either converge or diverge, facilitating the movement and balance of energy throughout the body.

It is essential to understand that Nadis are not physical nerves but energetic pathways through which Prana flows. Prana, derived from Sanskrit, is often translated as "life force" or "vital energy," though its essence is beyond a precise definition in words. This invisible, all-encompassing force sustains life in every living being, similar to how electricity powers devices or how wind propels the sails of a boat. Prana energizes us on a much deeper level, fueling not just our physical vitality but also mental clarity, emotional well-being, and spiritual awareness.

The human body operates using three primary types of energy: chemical, electrical, and pranic. Chemical energy, derived from nutrients in food, provides the fuel for all cellular processes through the conversion into adenosine triphosphate (ATP). Electrical energy, crucial for the nervous system, enables nerve impulses and brain functions. This form of energy was scientifically observed quite late in human history, with the invention of the ECG by Willem Einthoven in 1903 and the EEG by Hans Berger in 1924, measuring the electrical activity of the heart and brain, respectively.

While chemical energy powers the body and electrical energy drives neural functions, Pranic energy sustains our very life essence, bridging the physical and the metaphysical. Unlike chemical or electrical energy, which operate within measurable physical realms, Prana exists at the intersection of the tangible and intangible. It governs not just physiological functions but also our emotions, mental clarity, and spiritual awareness. Flowing through the Nadis, Pranic energy accumulates in the chakras, which act as regulators and distributors of this subtle force throughout the body. Balancing Pranic energy is crucial to maintaining vitality, focus, and resilience in life, much like maintaining harmony in the other energy systems.

Just as the breath provides the body with oxygen, Prana supplies a subtler form of nourishment. It energizes every action, thought, and emotion, connecting the mind and body while maintaining harmony with the external environment. The movement of Prana, orchestrated by the chakras, ensures the free flow of this vital energy for holistic health and well-being. This intricate interplay of chemical, electrical, and pranic energies highlights the complexity of the human system, where the chakras serve as conduits, harmonizing these forces into a cohesive flow that sustains life and elevates consciousness.

The seven chakras are dynamic hubs of energy that influence various facets of our well-being:

1. Muladhara (Root Chakra) – Foundation and stability.
2. Swadhisthana (Sacral Chakra) – Creativity and innovation.
3. Manipura (Solar Plexus Chakra) – Confidence and leadership.
4. Anahata (Heart Chakra) – Compassion and connection.
5. Vishuddha (Throat Chakra) – Communication and expression.
6. Ajna (Third Eye Chakra) – Intuition and vision.
7. Sahasrara (Crown Chakra) – Awareness and self-realization.

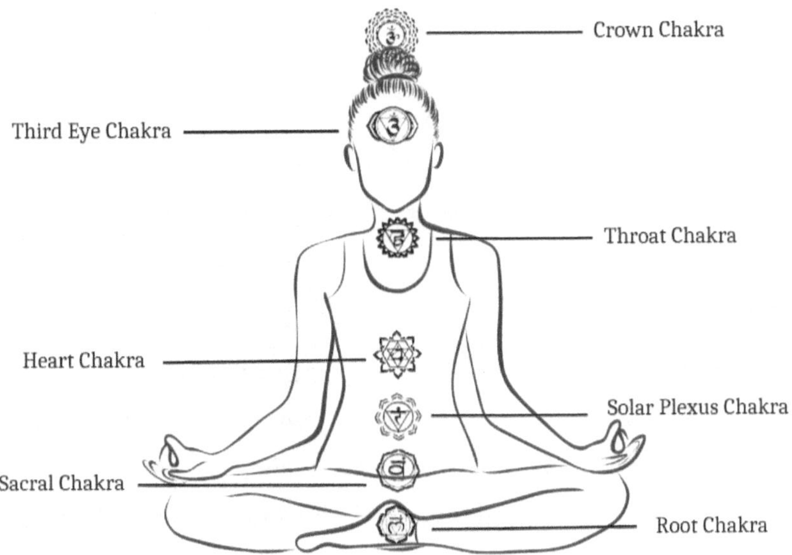

These chakras work in tandem to harmonize the flow of energy, influencing our physical, emotional, and mental states. To bridge the ancient wisdom of chakras with the modern world of business, consider the chakras as integral components that influence the core aspects of organizational success. Just as each chakra regulates specific energies in the body, businesses also thrive on the seamless flow of different energies—strategy, creativity, leadership, innovation, or execution. When one energy center falters in a person, it disrupts the flow of vitality; similarly, when one key area in a business is misaligned, the ripple effects can hinder the entire organization's progress.

Each chakra corresponds to a unique dimension of business functionality. For instance, the Root Chakra relates to establishing a strong foundation through vision and strategy, while the Sacral Chakra resonates with creativity and innovation. The Solar Plexus Chakra energizes leadership and confidence, driving purposeful action. These energy centers offer a framework for understanding and addressing the dynamic aspects of business operations. By synchronizing these "energy hubs," businesses can create a harmonious ecosystem where employees, leaders, and stakeholders thrive, fostering sustainable success.

Much like transport hubs, chakras regulate the flow of Prana, influencing physical health, emotional stability, and spiritual growth. Each of the seven chakras has a specific role, yet they are interconnected, forming a unified energy system. When one of these centers is disrupted, it causes a ripple effect, leading to imbalances in our physical, emotional, or mental state.

Without energy, a human body would be little more than an inert collection of elements and compounds. Similarly, a business without energy is merely a collection of property, plant, equipment, and furniture—lacking vitality or purpose. Just as the balanced flow of energy through the chakras ensures harmony between the mind and body, in business, energy brings cohesion to the systems, processes, and people that drive it. This energy transforms static assets into dynamic entities, where property, equipment, and infrastructure synergize seamlessly with the creativity, passion, and purpose of the people operating within them.

As we explore each chakra in the following sections, it is important to recognize that their attributes often overlap and interconnect, much like the multifaceted energies within a thriving organization. Each chakra, with its unique qualities and focus, influences various dimensions of our well-being. Similarly, in business, distinct energies converge to create a harmonious flow, ensuring that every facet contributes to the larger purpose and mission.

Muladhara
(The Root Chakra)

The word Muladhara (*moo-lah-dah-ruh*) is derived from the Sanskrit roots: "Mula," meaning root or base, and "Adhara," meaning support or foundation. Together, Muladhara signifies the "Root Support," emphasizing the foundational role this chakra plays in our physical and psychological well-being. Just like the roots of a tree, the Muladhara Chakra is responsible for our sense of grounding, stability, and security, providing us with the strength to withstand life's challenges.

Thus, Muladhara metaphorically represents the base upon which the entire energy system (or chakra system) stands. Just like a tree needs strong roots to stay grounded and grow, the Muladhara chakra provides the stability and grounding necessary for one's physical and psychological well-being.

Let us explore the key attributes of the Muladhara Chakra:

Grounding

The Muladhara is the foundation of our being, keeping us connected to the earth and grounded in reality. It provides stability, helping us build resilience and the strength to face challenges. Just as an individual relies on the grounding energy of the root chakra to feel secure, stable, and connected to the material world, a business must also establish a firm foundation that ensures stability in its operations.

In business, grounding refers to being firmly anchored in a clear, well-defined strategy that aligns with the company's mission and values. Without this connection to its core purpose, a business risks losing direction, much like an individual who lacks grounding may feel disoriented or insecure. A business must also establish a robust operational framework to support its vision—one that enables smooth functioning and adaptability in the face of external challenges, such as market shifts or economic downturns.

For instance, the Business Model Canvas, developed by Alexander Osterwalder, is a practical tool that reflects the grounding nature of a business. It lays out the fundamental building blocks—such as customer segments, value propositions, and key activities—ensuring that the business remains connected to its foundational goals, just as the root chakra keeps individuals grounded to their essential needs. This interconnectedness between a business's strategy and operational framework mirrors the stability and security that the root chakra provides for an individual.

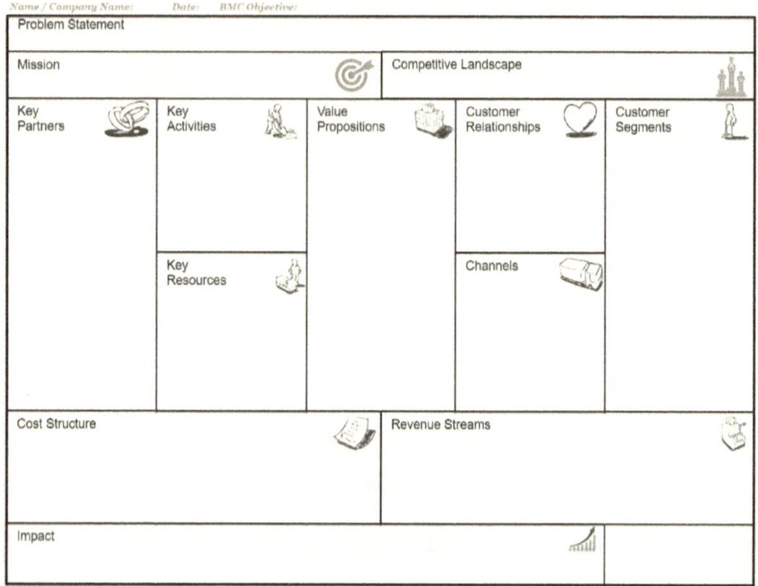

Survival

The Muladhara governs our basic survival instincts, ensuring we have the essentials for life, such as food, shelter, and a sense of safety. When this chakra is balanced, it gives us a secure foundation from which we can handle life's challenges, enabling us to feel confident and capable in meeting our needs.

For businesses, survival relies on securing core necessities such as steady revenue streams, a loyal customer base, and a sustainable cost structure—all integral components of the Business Model Canvas. These elements allow businesses to thrive even during difficult times. As Michael E. Gerber explains in his book *The E-Myth Revisited*, "The system—whether it be the business system, the education system, or any other—must be constructed to ensure survival and adaptability." Gerber emphasizes that well-defined processes and systems are critical to ensuring that a business can operate independently of its founder and maintain resilience.

The Business Model Canvas reinforces this survival strategy by ensuring businesses maintain clarity on how revenue is generated and which customer segments to prioritize, helping them navigate market fluctuations effectively. This mirrors the Muladhara's grounding function, providing both personal and organizational strength to remain stable in uncertain environments.

Vitality and Resilience

The Muladhara is the anchor of our physical and emotional well-being. It governs our body's essential functions—our bones, muscles, and adrenal glands—that contribute to our stress response and vitality. When this chakra is balanced, it empowers us to feel secure, grounded, and able to face life's challenges with resilience and stability.

In a business context, vitality translates to operational health. Just as a person needs strong bones and a balanced stress response, a business must maintain its core assets—financial, human capital, and technological—to function effectively. These assets act as the "lifeblood" of the organization, ensuring that the business can adapt to both expected and unexpected challenges.

Resilience, both for individuals and businesses, is the ability to withstand challenges and grow stronger as a result. As Brené Brown, a renowned researcher on courage and vulnerability, puts it, "You can choose courage or you can choose comfort, but you cannot choose both." This principle applies to businesses, especially in a rapidly changing world, where adaptability is key to thriving in the face of uncertainty.

Nassim Nicholas Taleb's seminal work adds a layer of depth to our understanding of resilience. In his book *The Black Swan: The Impact of the Highly Improbable*, Taleb explains how unpredictable, high-impact events—what he calls Black Swans—can completely upend expectations and shake industries. These events, such as economic crises, technological disruptions, or pandemics, are difficult to foresee, but their impact can be immense. Businesses, like individuals, must be prepared not only to withstand such shocks but to adapt and grow stronger in their wake.

Taleb extends this idea in his follow-up book, *Antifragile: Things That Gain from Disorder*. Taleb argues that it is not enough to simply be resilient in the face of adversity. Instead, systems—whether personal, business, or societal—should aim to thrive under pressure. Antifragile systems become stronger through stress and challenges, adapting and evolving rather than merely returning to their previous state. This concept applies directly to businesses that want to succeed in today's volatile and unpredictable markets. As Taleb notes, "Some things benefit from shocks; they thrive and grow when exposed to volatility, randomness, disorder, and stressors."

For businesses, this means developing robust systems that not only survive but also gain from unpredictable challenges. A strong, adaptable business foundation is crucial for navigating "black swan" events and emerging stronger, much like the Muladhara grounds us and enables us to handle life's unpredictability.

By embracing the principles of vitality and resilience—and moving toward the idea of becoming antifragile—we can build a foundation that not only withstands challenges but thrives under pressure. Having built resilience, the next step is to channel this energy into purposeful action through manifestation.

Manifestation

Manifestation begins with energy—everything, even thinking, requires energy before action can take place. Before any action is carried out, we must first envision it. The Muladhara, channels the energy that helps transform thoughts into reality. It is this energy that moves us from intention to action, driving our ideas forward.

In business, manifestation is about turning well-defined ideas into tangible results. A strong Value Proposition serves as the core of this process. It identifies what a business offers and how it solves its customers' problems. Without a clear value proposition, businesses risk stalling in the idea phase. Tools like the Business Model Canvas, irrespective of the size of a business, are essential for organizing resources and strategies to ensure a smooth translation of ideas into products, services, or outcomes that create value.

One of my all-time favorite books, Stephen Covey's *The 7 Habits of Highly Effective People*, brilliantly captures the essence of manifestation through his principle that "all things are created twice." The first creation is mental, where we envision our goals, and the second is the physical creation, where those ideas take shape in reality. This same principle applies to business: manifestation begins with clarity of purpose and continues through consistent execution to bring that vision to life.

Businesses like Howard Schultz's Starbucks exemplify this process. Schultz did not just envision selling coffee; he mentally created a space where people could connect—a "third place" between home and work—and then brought this idea to life, shaping Starbucks into a global phenomenon.

Vision must be coupled with decisive action for real progress. As Thomas Edison aptly put it, "Vision without action is hallucination," and without vision, action becomes mere exertion. For businesses, the key to success lies in uniting both—where a clear vision drives purposeful action, leading to long-term growth and success.

———————

Energetic Takeaways: Muladhara

1. Foundational Energy: Muladhara represents the energy of strong foundations, establishing robust principles like mission, values, and structure.
2. Protective Energy: Muladhara's energy of protection ensures resource security and financial stability.
3. Growth-Oriented Energy: A balanced Muladhara fosters an environment for enabling sustainable growth and expansion.

The Muladhara Matrix below visually represents how foundational energy, balanced and unbalanced, interacts with growth-oriented and foundational focus in a business. Use it as a guide to understand and address the energy dynamics within your organization:

Swadhisthana (The Sacral Chakra)

The Swadhisthana (*svah-dhee-stah-nuh*), or Sacral Chakra, is located just near the genitals. It governs the flow of creative and emotional energy within the body, playing a crucial role in our ability to experience pleasure, sensuality, and intimacy. This chakra is closely linked to our capacity for emotional expression and creative engagement with the world around us. The term "Swadhisthana" also comes from Sanskrit, where "Swa" means "self," and "Adhishthana" refers to "dwelling" or "seat," symbolizing this chakra as the residence of one's true inner self and creativity.

Let us explore the different attributes of the Swadhisthana Chakra:

Creativity

Creativity is the driving force behind innovation, and it finds its energy source in the Swadhisthana Chakra, which governs our ability to think beyond traditional structures. This chakra fuels our capacity to generate new ideas and transform concepts into reality, making it the heart of innovation. In both life and business, tapping into this creative energy is essential for bringing fresh, dynamic solutions to the forefront.

In business, Design Thinking captures the essence of creativity through its five steps: Empathize, Define, Ideate, Prototype, and Test. Each phase builds upon the other, encouraging teams to deeply understand user needs, articulate problems, brainstorm solutions, create prototypes, and rigorously test them. The Empathize phase, in particular, emphasizes understanding users' emotions and struggles to drive meaningful insights. Examples like Simon Sinek's *Start with Why*, which focuses on fulfilling emotional needs, and Airbnb's, user-centered approach illustrates how empathy catalyzes innovation by focusing on meaningful travel experiences and opportunities for connection.

Dyson, for example, famously went through over 5,000 prototypes before developing the bagless vacuum cleaner that revolutionized the household appliance market. This was not just creativity in the artistic sense, but creativity in problem-solving—a process of continual ideation, refinement, and testing, much like the fluid energy of the sacral chakra driving innovation.

The sacral chakra's creative energy also finds resonance in companies like Spotify, which disrupted the music industry through creative rethinking of how people access music. By embracing the idea of renting (streaming) rather than owning music (buying CDs or downloads), Spotify created a service that addressed multiple pain points for both users and artists, fundamentally altering the way people consume music. In the process, it eliminated music piracy, the scourge that dampened the spirits and threatened the livelihoods of professional musicians.

The Ideation Phase encourages this type of boundary-pushing thinking by encouraging teams to approach challenges from different angles. As David Kelley and Tom Kelley of IDEO emphasize, creativity is not just about coming up with wild ideas but is about giving yourself permission to think freely, uninhibited by conventional limitations. Their book, *Creative Confidence*, highlights how anyone can tap into this energy to foster innovation, much like how the sacral chakra fuels boundless creativity.

Creativity in businesses is not only about artistic expression but about challenging traditional solutions and driving innovation through imaginative thinking. Just as the sacral chakra's energy inspires individuals to think creatively, businesses that nurture creativity—especially in ideation processes—can unlock breakthroughs that propel them toward sustained success.

Sensuality

Sensuality is our ability to fully engage with the world through the senses. It is appreciating and experiencing the world through touch, taste, smell, sight, and sound.

Sensuality can be a pleasurable and fulfilling aspect of life, and it can be enjoyed in many different ways. This too requires energy to flourish. The Swadhisthana Chakra governs this flow of energy, enabling us to experience beauty, pleasure, and emotional connection with our surroundings. In a business context, this sensual energy is critical not only for product design but also for creating work environments that inspire creativity, emotional well-being and hence productivity.

The physical workplace or home plays a pivotal role in channeling sensual energy. One of the key Yogic principles related to spaces is Vastu, an ancient architectural science designed to harmonize the five elements—water, fire, earth, air, and space—within physical environments. Simplified, Vastu associates specific directions with these elements: Southeast for fire, Southwest for earth, Northwest for air, Northeast for water, and the center for space. For example, placing an electrical transformer, symbolizing fire, in the Northeast instead of the Southeast can create disharmony.

Vastu Living by Kathleen Cox, a favorite book of mine, has profoundly explored how homes and workplaces are designed with Vastu principles. Kathleen, a New Yorker has perhaps done more research on the subject than traditional Vastu pandits. Similar to the Chinese concept of Feng Shui, Vastu aims to shape the character and destiny of a property's occupants by channeling energies effectively. It's no wonder that modern, progressive workplaces are moving beyond sterile functionality to reflect the values and character of the organization, creating immersive, sensory-rich environments that inspire and energize.

Historically, offices and workspaces were designed with minimal consideration for aesthetics or employee well-being. Office design was often hierarchical: junior employees were confined to sparse, functional desks, while executive offices sometimes bordered on opulence, reflecting power and authority rather than creativity. Factories were even more detached from sensuality, often becoming sweatshops—dreary, mechanized environments with little regard for the well-being of their workers. Many factories, even today, are dominated by monotonous machinery, offering nothing to stimulate the senses of those working there.

However, the 21st century brought a revolution in how workplaces are designed. Instead of just being functional, they began to reflect the business's ethos, designed to inspire employees and create a more productive and positive atmosphere. The trend of designing workspaces to reflect a company's values began with pioneering firms like Google, which introduced vibrant, playful office environments in Mountain View, California, aimed at fostering creativity and collaboration among employees. Their open spaces, unconventional meeting rooms, and recreational areas broke away from the traditional, rigid office layouts. Likewise, Apple Park, located in Cupertino, California, epitomizes Apple's brand ethos through its sleek, minimalist architecture, designed to inspire innovation and elegance. Both companies set a new standard for how physical environments could mirror corporate philosophy and drive creative productivity.

In Europe, companies like Dille & Kamille stand out for incorporating their sustainability principles into the very design of their stores and offices. Their Utrecht office is an embodiment of simplicity, natural materials, and sustainability. The aesthetic choices are meant to harmonize with their ethos of environmentally friendly practices, from natural lighting to the use of wood and other sustainable materials. Every design decision reflects their commitment to environmental sustainability, resonating with their core values and attracting employees and visitors who share the same principles.

Similarly, the Kariwala facilities in India have been meticulously designed to stimulate the sensual energy of their employees, creating an environment that is not just functional but also inspiring. They have been crafted to reflect the company's values of sustainability and innovation, using natural elements, calming colors, and open spaces that encourage creativity and well-being. By incorporating aesthetics into the very fabric of the workspace, Kariwala ensures that employees remain connected to the company's mission of spreading happiness, and their energy is channeled toward creative and productive outcomes.

The origins of such character-rich workplaces lie in the idea that the environment in which we work profoundly affects our mood, creativity, and productivity. As philosopher Alain de Botton emphasizes in his book *The Architecture of Happiness*, the spaces we inhabit have the power to shape our emotional states. He notes that beautiful spaces, whether homes or offices, offer us a "promise of happiness," encouraging a more productive and joyful state of mind.

Psychological studies also support this connection. Dr. Nancy Etcoff, a cognitive psychologist at Harvard Medical School, has demonstrated that beauty and aesthetics are hardwired into the brain as tools for enhancing our survival and well-being. She explains that visually appealing spaces not only enhance mood but also lead to better cognitive function and focus. This research shows why companies investing in aesthetics are not only creating pleasant work environments but also boosting productivity and engagement.

As workplaces evolve, we now understand that aesthetic design is not just about appearances—it is about creating a holistic sensory experience that reflects the values and energy of the business. Companies like IKEA have designed their spaces to foster sustainability and functionality, mirroring their product offerings in their work environments. IKEA's sustainable building practices and emphasis on simplicity are reflected in their office designs, encouraging both employees and customers to live in harmony with those values.

This transformation in workplace design, whether in offices, stores, or factories, underscores the connection between sensual energy and business success. Sensuality in the workspace can significantly enhance creativity, engagement, and productivity, much like the Swadhisthana fuels emotional and creative expression in individuals. By investing in spaces that reflect their core values, businesses can create environments that not only function but also resonate emotionally with everyone who walks through their doors. As philosopher John O'Donohue once said, "The environment you create has the power to mold not just your physical experience, but your very soul."

Fertility

The Swadhisthana energizes fertility, representing the power to create and sustain life beyond just the physical sense. It energizes the desire to procreate and be responsible for a new life. In business it is to bring something new into the world—whether in the form of ideas, innovations, or entire businesses. This desire is fueled by energy, and it is this energetic potential that allows us to continuously evolve and grow.

In the context of business, fertility is the ability to generate new ventures and maintain long-term growth. This energy is closely linked to business growth, much like the concept of the growth mindset as opposed to fixed mindset in *Mindset* by Carol Dweck. Businesses need to embrace challenges and view them as opportunities for improvement, which ensures that they can remain innovative and relevant.

For example, Nintendo—originally founded in 1889 as a playing card company—repeatedly reinvented itself over the years. It expanded from producing traditional card games to becoming a global leader in the video game industry, driven by its relentless pursuit of innovation and growth. Nintendo's ability to recognize new opportunities and create groundbreaking products like the Game Boy and Nintendo Switch illustrates how fertile companies can thrive in changing markets.

Similarly, LEGO, initially a wooden toy company, faced a downturn in the early 2000s. Instead of succumbing to market pressures, it leveraged its creative energy to reinvent itself. By introducing LEGO Mindstorms (a robotics toolkit) and partnering with entertainment franchises like Star Wars, LEGO became a global leader in creative play, demonstrating how fertile businesses can transform challenges into opportunities for sustained success.

Energetic Takeaways: Swadhisthana

1. Creative Energy: Swadhisthana embodies the energy of creativity, enabling innovative solutions and fostering design thinking within teams.
2. Adaptive Energy: The fluidity of Swadhisthana inspires adaptability, helping businesses thrive amidst changing market dynamics.
3. Collaborative Energy: This energy promotes harmony and co-creation, encouraging inclusive ideation and stronger teamwork.

The Swadhisthana Matrix visually represents how creative and adaptive energies, whether balanced or unbalanced, interact within the context of business dynamics. Use it as a guide to enhance innovation, adaptability, and collaboration in your organization.

Manipura
(The Solar Plexus Chakra)

The Manipura (*munny-poora*), or Solar Plexus Chakra, is located just above the navel and is often referred to as the "Abode of Jewels." It draws its name from the Sanskrit roots "Mani," meaning "jewel," and "Pura," meaning "city" or "abode," symbolizing the center of personal power, self-confidence, and vitality. This chakra energizes our sense of personal identity, self-esteem, and emotional regulation, and it is responsible for giving us the inner strength to take decisive action, lead with confidence, and handle life's challenges with resilience. We often use expressions like "got the guts," "gut-feel," or "butterflies in the stomach" without realizing that these phrases directly point to the solar plexus region. This area is not only central to these sensations but also to intuitive experiences, underscoring its connection to courage, instinct, and emotional response.

Let us explore the key attributes of this very important Chakra:

Confidence

The Manipura serves as the seat of personal power, self-confidence, and decisiveness. It energizes our capacity to lead with conviction, make assertive decisions, and project our inner strength into the world. When this chakra is balanced, we can navigate life's challenges with confidence, fully aware of our inner potential and power.

In a business context, this energy translates into personal branding and leadership, which are essential to driving success in a competitive landscape. Entrepreneurs and leaders who harness the power of the Manipura not only exude personal confidence but also fuel the growth of their businesses through authentic self-expression.

Take Satya Nadella, for example. His bold vision for Microsoft illustrates how a deep well of confidence, akin to the Manipura's energy, enables him to take calculated risks and push the boundaries of innovation. Nadella has built a personal brand that reflects empathy, vision, and a relentless drive to empower others—qualities that energize his leadership. His focus on growth, inclusivity, and purpose has inspired confidence not only among his employees, investors, and customers but also in the tech industry at large. Under his leadership, Microsoft has transformed into a global leader in cloud computing and artificial intelligence. Interestingly, despite his high-profile position, Nadella remains grounded, focusing on long-term vision while fostering a culture of collaboration and resilience across the organization.

Similarly, Anand Mahindra, chairman of the Mahindra Group, and Richard Branson, founder of the Virgin Group, offer compelling examples of leaders who channel the energy of the Manipura into their personal and professional brands. Mahindra masterfully uses social media to project his brand of leadership, intertwining personal values with innovation, ethics, and business transformation. This approach fosters authenticity and trust, creating a direct connection between him and the Mahindra Group—extending his influence beyond the boardroom to customers and stakeholders. Likewise, Branson's adventurous spirit, confidence, and daring personality are intrinsic to the Virgin Group's success across diverse industries, from airlines to music. By projecting values of adventure, fun, and boldness, Branson exemplifies how energized leaders take bold steps that elevate not only themselves but their entire organizations.

What was once looked down upon as narcissism is now viewed as personal branding—a strategic approach in today's business landscape. Leaders who integrate their identity and authenticity with the mission of their business build meaningful connections with employees and customers, though the jury is still out on whether this can always lead to long-term success. The energy from the Manipura fuels this trust, inspiring others and creating a ripple effect that enhances organizational performance and loyalty.

Emotional Regulation

The Manipura helps regulate emotions, allowing us to manage feelings such as anger, fear, and frustration with composure. A balanced chakra fosters emotional equilibrium, leading to inner peace and control over outward reactions. This emotional balance is crucial in leadership, where effective leaders not only manage their own emotions but also those of their teams.

Daniel Goleman, in his groundbreaking book *Emotional Intelligence: Why It Can Matter More Than IQ*, brought attention to the critical role that emotional intelligence (EI) plays in leadership and professional success. Goleman highlights that self-regulation, empathy, and social awareness—core components of EI—are key in creating harmonious work environments. Emotional Intelligence refers to an individual's ability to perceive, assess, and manage emotions effectively.

While IQ measures cognitive abilities, EQ quantifies emotional intelligence, capturing an individual's capacity to handle interpersonal dynamics. High EQ in leaders fosters trust and resilience within teams, creating an environment where employees feel heard and supported. Emotional regulation, a key aspect of EQ, is not about suppressing negative emotions but harnessing them productively—turning potential disruptions into opportunities for growth and fostering a culture where both challenges and successes are handled with poise.

Assertiveness

At the heart of the Manipura lies assertiveness—the ability to project authority and lead with conviction while maintaining humility. This chakra empowers individuals to assert themselves in a way that is commanding yet respectful, enabling them to make decisive, strategic choices while remaining open to feedback and collaboration. Such balanced leadership drives both effectiveness and compassion.

One prominent example is Indra Nooyi, the former CEO of PepsiCo, who embodied a powerful blend of assertiveness and empathy. During her tenure, Nooyi steered the company's global expansion and introduced healthier product options, marking a significant shift from its traditional focus on soda and snacks. Her leadership style, as detailed in her book *My Life in Full*, combined strategic decisiveness with emotional intelligence, earning her widespread respect both within and outside the organization. Nooyi often emphasized the importance of asking insightful questions to guide her team effectively, showcasing a thoughtful and collaborative approach to leadership.

Assertiveness is not about dominating conversations or silencing others' input. Instead, as Daniel Goleman highlights in his follow-up book *Leadership That Gets Results*, it combines decisiveness with an open-minded attitude. Goleman's research demonstrates that leaders who blend assertiveness with empathy—two fundamental elements of emotional intelligence—drive performance and foster innovation more effectively than those who rely purely on authority.

Determination

The Manipura is the wellspring of determination and perseverance. It fuels the inner drive to overcome obstacles and to push forward with unyielding energy. This attribute differentiates people who merely survive from those who thrive under pressure.

A good example is the unrelenting determination of Howard Schultz, the former CEO of Starbucks. Despite facing numerous challenges, including skepticism from investors and the difficulty of scaling his vision for a coffeehouse brand, Schultz's belief in his mission and relentless pursuit of growth ultimately turned Starbucks into one of the most recognized brands in the world. His perseverance and grit have been key to his success and continue to inspire entrepreneurs everywhere.

The book *Grit: The Power of Passion and Perseverance* by Angela Duckworth highlights that success depends more on determination than talent alone. This concept reflects the energy of the Manipura, which enables us to stay the course even when faced with significant challenges. This chakra energizes businesses with the strength to persevere, to adapt and grow in the marketplace. Determination fuels resilience, key to long-term sustainability in a VUCA world.

Direction

The Manipura is intimately linked to our sense of direction in life, enabling us to direct our actions toward our long-term goals. When this chakra is balanced, individuals feel a clear sense of direction. A huge amount of energy is required to know the direction one is headed, both physically and metaphorically. Without this inner compass, we are at risk of drifting aimlessly, much like what Lewis Carroll famously said, "If you don't know where you're going, any road will take you there." The Manipura provides the directive energy to navigate challenges and remain steadfast, ensuring focus amidst distractions.

In a business, the scarcest resource is the time of its CEO. The most effective leaders prioritize their energy on steering the organization in the right direction rather than becoming engrossed in the 'daily grind'. They focus their time and resources on balancing the company's vision with its actions. There is nothing so useless as doing efficiently that which should not be done at all.

It is no coincidence that board members are called directors in a company. Their primary responsibility is to ensure that the business stays on course, staying true to its mission and values. They do not engage in the minutiae of everyday operations but instead preserve their energy for strategic decisions that keep the organization headed in the right direction. As Peter Drucker said, "Efficiency is doing things right; effectiveness is doing the right things." The Manipura energizes this balance.

The concept of heroic versus post-heroic leadership, introduced by scholars Ronald Heifetz and James MacGregor Burns, draws a key distinction between leaders who strive to be the solution for every problem and those who focus on empowering others to solve the problem. Heroic leaders often respond reactively, focusing on immediate solutions. In contrast, post-heroic leaders prioritize developing systems and empowering their teams, ensuring the organization remains aligned with its long-term goals. Counter-intuitively, the greatest risk a leader faces is to become a hero!

Mukesh Ambani of Reliance Industries, has consistently demonstrated how *not* to be a hero. Under his direction, Reliance has undergone strategic shifts, particularly with the launch of Jio, which disrupted the Indian telecom market and transformed the digital landscape of the country. Ambani's foresight and ability to steer his company in new directions—away from its traditional sectors and into telecommunications and digital services—highlights how a well-defined path is essential for long-term success. By focusing on the future direction rather than the management of his businesses, Ambani ensures that Reliance remains adaptable and forward-thinking to thrive in the VUCA world today.

Many companies bring in independent directors to provide an external perspective. This approach embodies the guiding energy of the Manipura, akin to being a "Drishta," a vital concept in Yogic philosophy. A Drishta (a seer) observes without attachment, maintaining clarity and ensuring purpose.

This concept is a subject unto itself in Yogic philosophy. Hence, I have added an outline as an appendix for those who wish to dive deeper.

Energetic Takeaways: Manipura

1. Empowering Energy: Manipura represents confidence and self-worth, driving effective leadership and decisive action in business.
2. Motivational Energy: The fire of Manipura fuels ambition and passion, inspiring teams to work towards shared goals.
3. Resilient Energy: This energy builds the capacity to face challenges, fostering strength and adaptability in overcoming obstacles.

The Manipura Matrix illustrates the interplay between balanced and unbalanced energies in leadership and team focus, helping businesses harness confidence, motivation, and clarity for greater impact.

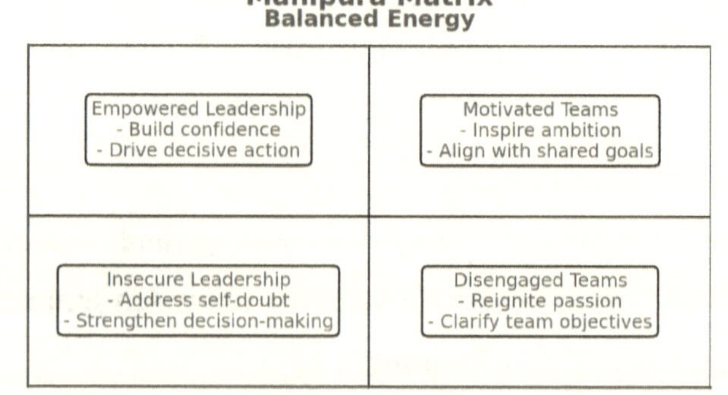

Anahata
(The Heart Chakra)

Anahata (*un-aa-hata*) derived from the Sanskrit roots 'un' and 'ahata', translates to "unstruck" or "unbeaten". This reflects the Heart Chakra's essence as a center of unconditional love, compassion, and balance. Located in the center of the chest, Anahata is the heart's energetic counterpart, distinct from the physical heart on the left. It serves as the core that energizes our ability to connect with others, give and receive love, and experience emotional harmony.

The Anahata or the Heart Chakra is associated with empathy, kindness, and acceptance. When activated, it allows us to navigate relationships with openness, forgiveness, and depth. This chakra's energy creates the physical sensation we feel in moments of love or empathy—a deep, heart-centered resonance that connects us with the people and world around us. An energized Anahata empowers us to engage in meaningful relationships, compassion, and maintain emotional balance.

Let us examine the key attributes of the Anahata:

Love and Compassion

The Anahata is the energetic source of love and compassion, qualities that inspire a genuine concern for the well-being of others. In the realm of business and leadership, these qualities form the foundation of a healthy work culture, enabling teams to connect on a human level and work harmoniously. Compassion requires emotional capacity, which, when nurtured, creates an environment where individuals feel valued, accepted, and psychologically safe. It does not mean tolerating poor performance. Accountability remains important. The key is whether there is room for honest reflection on mistakes, allowing the organization to grow and learn from them.

The concept of psychological safety, introduced by Amy Edmondson of Harvard Business School, highlights creating environments where employees feel comfortable taking risks and expressing themselves without fear of criticism or punishment. Edmondson's research shows that compassion, energized by the Heart Chakra, helps foster open communication, risk-taking, and creativity, enabling teams to innovate freely.

Compassion in business decision-making bridges logic with the emotional intelligence necessary for sound, values-driven choices. Baba Shiv of Stanford University highlights that most decisions are driven by the emotional brain and only later validated by logic. For years, I carried a sense of guilt about thinking from the heart rather than the head. It was not until I opened up to fellow leaders that I realized how universal this is. They, too, often made emotional decisions first, rationalizing them afterward. Knowing this felt like finding my tribe—a shared understanding that we are all navigating this balance. Leaders who integrate compassion into decision-making create choices that not only reinforce core values but also support long-term vision and sustainable outcomes.

Relationships

At the core of the Anahata lies the energy to build and nurture meaningful relationships. In personal life, these relationships provide emotional support, security, and a sense of belonging. In the business realm, cultivating genuine relationships promotes collaboration, loyalty, and long-term commitment. This concept is explored deeply in Dr. Dharius Daniels' book *Relational Intelligence* and Adam Grant's *Give and Take*. Daniels defines relational intelligence as the skill of discerning, nurturing, and sustaining connections with purpose, while Grant focuses on building trust and cooperation through authentic, non-transactional connections. In effect, these perspectives underscore the importance of understanding and investing in relationships to foster trust, loyalty, and mutual respect.

Relationally intelligent leaders actively invest in understanding their team members' unique qualities and motivations, creating workplaces where individuals feel valued and supported. This approach drives loyalty, collaboration, and resilience within teams, enhancing both individual and organizational success.

Forgiveness

Hollywood and Bollywood have long glamorized revenge and redemption, elevating these concepts to heroic, glamorous ideals. However, successful leaders often take a different approach, understanding that not every battle is worth fighting and that energy is better invested in forgiveness and strategic focus. Forgiving—whether a delinquent employee, a defaulting client, or even a usurping competitor—requires substantial emotional energy drawn from the Anahata Chakra but often pays dividends in clarity, focus, and maintaining momentum toward larger goals.

Forgiveness in business is not about passivity or weakness. It involves letting go of anger and resentment to conserve energy for more productive outcomes. Personally, forgiveness has been one of my greatest challenges. I used to clutch anger like a burning coal, hoping it would harm the object of my resentment—only to realize, as time and greying hairs taught me, that it was my own hand being scorched. Strategic leaders understand that every fight is not necessary to win the war. In *The Art of War* by Sun Tzu, the importance of carefully choosing battles is emphasized, ensuring focus remains on what truly matters. Leaders who forgive effectively take corrective actions without letting personal vendettas interfere, embodying a calm and measured approach to challenges.

Dr. Robin Casarjian's book *Forgiveness* provides insights into how letting go can be a path to emotional healing and personal growth. It is an easy read that offers practical wisdom for leaders and individuals alike. The practice of forgiveness allows us to channel our energy productively, ensuring resilience and the ability to focus on long-term goals.

Letting go and giving up are fundamentally different. Forgiveness should also be distinguished from pacifism. Unchecked leniency risks being mistaken for weakness. Leaders understand that while forgiveness can be a powerful tool, appropriate boundaries and consequences must still be in place. Exemplary actions can deter future offenses without compromising energy or integrity. As the adage goes, behavior that gets rewarded gets repeated. Conversely, inappropriate behavior left unaddressed often becomes a pattern, not just for the individual but for others who observe it. The key lies in finding balance. This balance between forgiveness and accountability fosters both integrity and trust within teams and organizations.

Energetic Takeaways: Anahata

1. Compassionate Energy: Anahata embodies empathy and understanding, fostering meaningful connections and harmonious relationships in business.
2. Harmonizing Energy: This energy balances emotional intelligence with rational decision-making, creating a stable and productive work environment.
3. Inspirational Energy: The openness of Anahata inspires trust and collaboration, enabling teams to thrive and innovate together.

The Anahata Matrix showcases how empathetic and collaborative energies, whether balanced or unbalanced, influence leadership and team dynamics to create harmony and trust in the workplace.

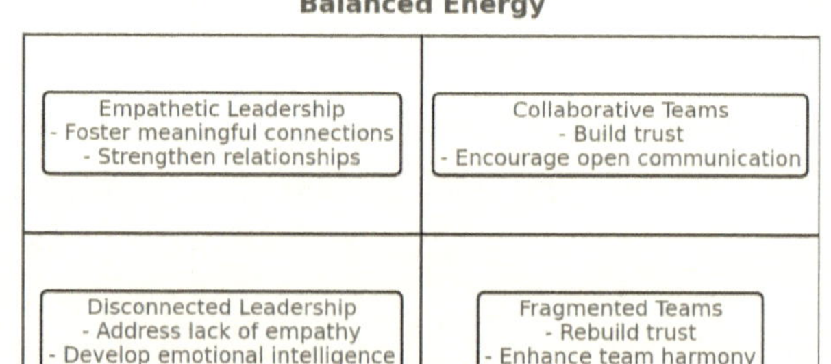

Vishuddha
(The Throat Chakra)

The Vishuddha (*vee-shood-dha*) derives its name from the Sanskrit roots "Vi" (meaning "fully") and "Shuddha" (meaning "pure"), combining to signify "fully pure" or "the purest." Situated at the throat, this chakra governs communication, olfactory senses, authenticity, and active listening. It is intricately connected to the ENT (Ear-Nose-Throat) regions of the body, enabling the ability to speak, hear, and process sound effectively. The Vishuddha empowers us to express our truths, ideas, and emotions with clarity and confidence. It nurtures authenticity by aligning words with actions and values while fostering active listening, which deepens understanding and engagement. These attributes collectively define the Vishuddha's essence of pure expression and meaningful connection.

Let us explore the key attributes of the Vishuddha:

Communication

Communication, the foremost attribute of the Vishuddha Chakra, extends beyond the simple transmission of information. Effective communication requires that one's intentions, ideas, and values are conveyed clearly and without distortion. And this requires a lot of energy. The single biggest problem in communication is the illusion that it has taken place. Misunderstandings frequently stem not from ill intentions but from ineffective communication.

In the realm of business, clear communication can make or break relationships and strategic initiatives. Philip Kotler's *Marketing 4.0* emphasizes the shift towards customer-centered communication, which relies on understanding and connecting with audiences authentically. This approach, centered on listening to customer needs, highlights that clear and transparent communication is essential in modern marketing. Content marketing exemplifies this shift, where businesses actively communicate with audiences rather than to them, focusing on building long-term relationships rather than achieving short-term gains.

For entrepreneurs, effectively communicating their big idea is crucial for building support and trust. Matt Abrahams of Stanford Graduate School of Business has three simple questions for any pitch: What? So what? Now what? Clear answers to these questions ensures salience, resonance and confidence in their vision.

On the other hand, poor communication often leads to significant failures. For instance, Nokia's decline as a mobile leader was partly due to internal miscommunication and a reluctance to challenge leadership on critical market shifts. Miscommunication also frequently results in industrial disputes, where employees feel neglected or misunderstood, undermining trust and efficiency.

Crucial Conversations by Joseph Grenny and his co-authors highlights the importance of open dialogue in resolving workplace conflicts and fostering a positive work environment. The book presents practical frameworks for handling challenging conversations with clarity and respect. Without the energy from a balanced Vishuddha, effective communication remains an elusive ideal.

Authenticity

Most of us grew up associating "washing" with laundry or cleaning cars—until we came across greenwashing, healthwashing, fairwashing, or pinkwashing. Now, "washing" often signifies a company's attempt to glitter without being the proverbial gold. Greenwashing is where businesses brand themselves as eco-friendly with scant regard for the environment. Pinkwashing is using LGBTQ+ messaging without genuinely supporting those initiatives. Fairwashing is claiming fair trade in a trade fair (pun intended) or healthwashing is selling sugar-laced natural 'health drinks'. And how did I forget the whitewashing politicians?

Cultures across the world have denounced this disharmony as Kathani vs. Karani (words vs. actions) in Hindi or Tatemae vs. Honne (facade vs. feelings) in Japanese or the Spanish proverb "Del dicho al hecho hay mucho trecho" that translates to "from saying to doing, there's a long stretch."

Authenticity, a core attribute of the energy from the Vishuddha Chakra, requires harmony between words, actions, and values. In the business landscape, this attribute is essential as consumers are increasingly adept at identifying contradictions. Authenticity demands more than just claiming values; it requires leaders to embody those values, fostering trust and credibility.

Many like me stopped paying a premium for the green credentials of Starbucks upon learning that their CEO commutes to work by private jet or started second-guessing those sustainability celebrities who travel to Davos in their barrage of private jets to discuss climate change at WEF. Sometimes, the punishments are far more severe. One such incident is known as the "Ratner Effect." In 1991, Gerald Ratner, CEO of Ratner's Group, jokingly called his own products "crap," causing an immediate public backlash. This single comment destroyed customer trust, wiping out £500 million in market value. Ratner's had to rebrand as Signet Group to recover, but the damage was irreversible.

And billions vanish when businesses lack authenticity. Theranos, founded by Elizabeth Holmes and once valued at $9 billion, crashed to nothing simply because their "blood tests" were not tests at all. It beats me how companies like Walgreens could form partnerships with them and investors queued up without running a 'test' on their 'tests.' Similarly, Sam Bankman-Fried (SBF) and his crypto exchange FTX serve as another glaring example. FTX, once one of the most respected cryptocurrency exchanges, attracted billions in investments. Ironically, SBF's promises of transparency and ethical leadership drew trust from global investors and customers. Yet, as investigations unfolded, it was revealed that FTX had been mismanaging customer funds, using them to prop up SBF's trading firm, Alameda Research. This mismatch between the *Kathani-Karani* of FTX caused $34 billion to evaporate overnight!

Speaking of crypto, I risk being labeled as uninformed, old-fashioned, or perhaps hopelessly skeptical for what I am about to share. I do not understand crypto! Not the technology behind it, but its very authenticity. It feels like a cryptograph I am yet to decipher, filled with questions that only deepen the mystery. For instance, if Bitcoin is mined by solving complex mathematical problems, why can't more problems be solved with increasing computing power? And what exactly are these problems? Then there is Willow, Google's latest quantum computing chip, capable of performing computations in "five minutes that would take supercomputers 10 septillion years." If Willow can do that, why can't it break the blockchain and multiply the supply? But who decided Bitcoin should be finite in the first place? If Bitcoin is finite, how come Dogecoin is not? Crypto remains a fascinating yet perplexing space. Until I find authentic understanding, I will keep my wallet closed to it. I have attempted to briefly explain this in Appendix 8: The Crypto *Mrigatrishna*.

Active Listening

Active listening, the third key attribute of the Vishuddha Chakra, involves more than empathy; it is a conscious effort to understand and engage with others. This attribute requires full presence and attention, validating the speaker's experience. As *The 7 Habits of Highly Effective People* by Stephen Covey highlights, "Seek first to understand, then to be understood." This is active listening and it requires a significant amount of energy that enables true understanding, fosters productive conversations, and minimizes conflict.

In a 360-degree review some time ago, my team gave me feedback that I do not actively listen. So often, we indeed can easily understand a problem even before it is fully stated. We interrupt and start offering the solution. Listening actively, even when not really required, requires a lot of energy that is channeled through the Vishuddha. When we listen attentively, we gain deeper insights and show respect to the speaker, encouraging them to share openly in the future. Unlike empathy, which centers on shared emotions, active listening focuses on understanding the speaker's message without preconceptions.

Active listening also enhances communication in negotiations and conflict resolution. In diplomacy, effective negotiators prioritize listening to opposing views, understanding the motivations and concerns of their counterparts. This attribute has parallels in the business world, where disputes often stem from miscommunication or a lack of understanding. Actively listening to grievances can resolve tensions before they escalate, promoting a harmonious work environment.

At Kariwala, we have cultivated a culture of listening to respond, not to react. For routine matters, a key practice we follow is asynchronous communication, which allows us to fully utilize the gap between stimulus and response. Instead of relying on phone calls or walk-up-to-desk interruptions, we encourage the use of Screenrecording videos like Loom, voice notes and instant messages for routine matters. This approach gives individuals the time to thoughtfully process information before crafting their response, avoiding the impulsiveness often associated with synchronous interactions. By embracing asynchronous communication, we ensure clarity, reduce interruptions, and foster intentional, well-considered dialogue across the organization.

Energetic Takeaways: Vishuddha

1. Expressive Energy: Vishuddha fosters clear and impactful communication, enabling us to articulate vision and goals effectively.

2. Authentic Energy: This energy emphasizes honesty and transparency, building trust and credibility in relationships.

3. Empowering Energy: The openness of Vishuddha inspires others by enabling a culture of listening and mutual respect.

The Vishuddha Matrix highlights the balance and imbalance in communication and relationship dynamics, offering insights to foster clarity, transparency, and trust in leadership and teams.

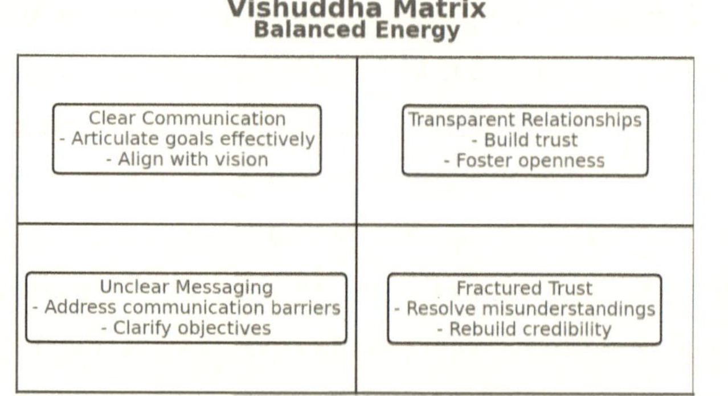

Ajna
(The Third Eye Chakra)

The Ajna Chakra, pronounced "Aagya" in Sanskrit, is situated near the pineal gland, between the eyebrows. Derived from the Sanskrit term meaning "command" or "perception," Ajna symbolizes insight and intuitive understanding. Often referred to as the Third Eye Chakra, it literally does what a third eye is supposed to do—foster intuition, foresight, and wisdom—essential traits for impactful leadership and strategic decision-making. When fully energized, this chakra enhances our ability to trust our instincts, foresee potential outcomes, and make clear, confident decisions that nurture both short and long-term goals.

Symbolized by a two-petaled lotus, *Ajna* represents the dual aspects of perception: rationality and intuition, the visible and the unseen, knowledge and wisdom. It serves as a portal to expanded awareness, allowing us to connect with a depth of insight that surpasses surface-level understanding. An activated Ajna Chakra grants clarity and focus, empowering us to harness our intuitive abilities, anticipate future possibilities, and make decisions that resonate with a balanced vision.

The essential attributes of this higher chakra include:

Intuition

The Ajna or Third Eye Chakra energizes intuition, empowering us to make visionary decisions that go beyond logic. Management literature increasingly recognizes that impactful decisions often arise from intuition rather than strictly data-driven approaches. Interestingly, decisions that appear deeply considered or data-based are sometimes intuitive leaps, later framed to fit logical narratives. This tendency is particularly evident among startup founders, whose initially "crazy" ideas often evolve into groundbreaking innovations.

Consider Mark Zuckerberg's creation of Facebook. Inspired by the concept that a person's face could "read like an open book," he trusted his intuition about the power of a social platform centered on personal connections. While the idea initially seemed improbable to many, his unwavering belief in its potential transformed Facebook into one of the world's most influential platforms.

Brian Chesky and Joe Gebbia, the founders of Airbnb, faced disbelief when they came up with the idea of strangers renting out their homes—or even just a room with an air mattress. The idea seemed not just unconventional but downright crazy. At a time when the notion of "sharing" one's home with strangers was virtually unheard of, traditional investors hesitated. Yet, Chesky and Gebbia trusted their intuition, sensing a demand for affordable and unique travel experiences. Their belief in their idea led to Airbnb, which revolutionized the hospitality industry and redefined how people travel worldwide.

Rent the Runway, now a unicorn, was founded by Jennifer Hyman and Jennifer Fleiss on what felt like an utterly impractical—even crazy—idea: renting out high-end designer clothes. Critics openly questioned why anyone, especially the wealthy, would rent clothes worn by others—a concept I personally still find baffling! Yet, Hyman and Fleiss followed their intuition, convinced there was a demand for "affordable luxury," a term that does feel like an oxymoron to me. Today, Rent the Runway has transformed retail, ushering in a culture of shared consumption and proving that the most counterintuitive ideas can often yield extraordinary success.

This chakra allows us to sense potential where others see uncertainty, transforming bold visions into actionable strategies. These examples illustrate how an activated Ajna Chakra enables us to trust unconventional, intuitive insights and turn ideas into reality. Paulo Coelho's words in The Alchemist, "Listen to your heart. It knows all things," capture the essence of this intuition. When balanced with clarity and vision, this intuitive focus empowers us to envision possibilities beyond the obvious, forging paths that others may not yet perceive.

Wisdom

Einstein's famous quote, "wisdom is not a product of schooling, but of the lifelong attempt to acquire it," very easily reflects the essence of the Ajna Chakra, which fosters wisdom and guides us to see beyond immediate concerns and understand the larger forces at play. Acquiring wisdom requires an immense amount of energy and an open mind. Wisdom is built upon a progression: data leads to information, information becomes knowledge, knowledge forms decisions, and ultimately, the outcome of decisions shape wisdom—completing a cycle back to refined data.

In *The Fifth Discipline* by Peter Senge, systems thinking is highlighted as a way to understand the interconnectedness of knowledge, reflecting the essence of wisdom in leadership. Senge emphasizes that true learning organizations cultivate wisdom by seeing beyond immediate issues and understanding the underlying structure of complex problems. Another relevant work, *Thinking, Fast and Slow* by Daniel Kahneman, shows how intuition and wisdom interact, underscoring the importance of both deep analysis and instinct in decision-making.

From these modern strategic guides to ancient philosophical texts—wisdom literature has been the bedrock of societies, shaping the collective understanding of ethics, purpose, and leadership. Though our individual bodies may only span a few decades, our genetic memory carries the legacy of wisdom passed down over thousands of years. An energized Ajna Chakra enables one to connect deeply with this accumulated knowledge within ourselves, inspiring us to draw upon timeless insights to make decisions that are grounded in centuries of human experience.

Reading wisdom literature is akin to distilling the author's lifetime of experience, learning in hours what took them years or even decades to accumulate. Personalities like Warren Buffett, Bill Gates, or Oprah Winfrey are known for their voracious reading habits, understanding that wisdom compounds just like wealth. They treat books as an investment in themselves and in their organizations, knowing that these insights guide better decision-making and foster true vision.

As Warren Buffett famously says, "The best investment you can make is an investment in yourself." This dedication to continual learning and wisdom is a habit among the most successful, yet it requires significant energy. Many find it challenging to absorb wisdom literature—often due to a blocked or imbalanced Ajna Chakra, which can impede focus and the desire to engage deeply with complex ideas. Energizing this chakra enables one to appreciate and internalize wisdom, allowing it to influence life and leadership in meaningful ways. Wisdom, in this sense, begets wisdom, as insights build upon one another, creating a virtuous cycle of learning, growth, and perspective.

Perception

Perception and intuition, though deeply interconnected, represent distinct facets of the Ajna Chakra. While intuition emerges as an inner compass, perception manifests as outward clarity—an unbiased lens through which we interpret the world around us. This quality of perception allows us to evaluate situations with precision, considering both immediate and long-term implications, free from personal biases or external pressures. An energized Ajna is vital for sustaining the high energy required to view complex situations with such clarity and neutrality.

Perceptive leaders possess an extraordinary ability to discern deeper truths. Steve Jobs exemplified this trait with his acute market perception. He famously observed, "People don't know what they want until you show it to them," highlighting how perceptive insight drives innovation. Similarly, Warren Buffett's unparalleled ability to perceive value enables him to uncover investment opportunities others might overlook, demonstrating the power of perception in strategic decision-making.

The significance of perception is explored in *Perception* by Dennis Proffitt and Drake Baer, which delves into the science behind how we interpret reality and its impact on decision-making. In *The Art of Perception*, Kate Colbert examines how leaders leverage perception to foster clarity and understanding in complex organizational contexts. Both works underscore that clear perception is indispensable for making wise decisions and navigating human dynamics.

By harnessing the energy of an activated Ajna, leaders gain the ability to filter noise from meaningful insights. In today's business landscape—often muddled by competing interests and short-term thinking—this heightened perception equips leaders to act with integrity, objectivity, and vision. An energized Ajna Chakra enables them to guide their teams with the clarity and balance necessary to thrive.

The Ajna Chakra and Business Growth: A Strategic Framework

The Ajna Chakra's attributes—Intuition, Wisdom, and Perception—are crucial for business growth. Channeled through leadership, these energies drive strategies that fuel revenue, profitability, innovation, market share, brand reputation, and adaptability, while mitigating risks through diversification. Growth is essential not only for businesses to thrive but also for non-profits to expand their impact. It is not the opposite of contentment; rather, the two are complementary. Growth represents improvement and expansion, while contentment stems from gratitude and acceptance. Together, they balance ambition with peace, ensuring sustainable and meaningful progress. Contentment prevents burnout, and growth prevents stagnation, fostering purpose in both personal and professional realms.

A structured approach to growth is captured in Igor Ansoff's renowned Ansoff Matrix. Ansoff, a mathematician and business theorist, is widely regarded as the father of strategic management. Below is the matrix and a table linking the Ajna Chakra's attributes to each quadrant:

Ansoff Matrix

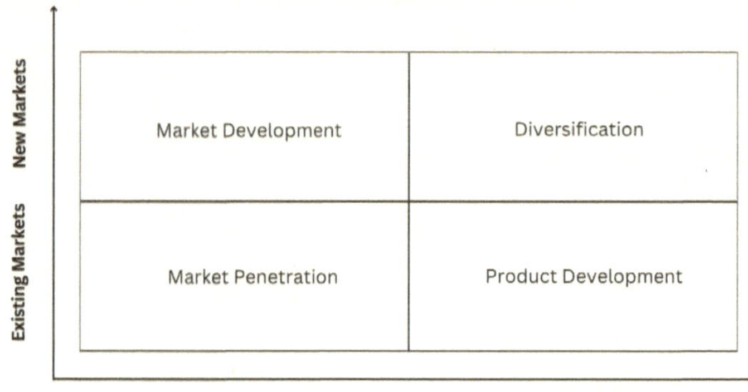

Quadrant	Attribute	Focus	Description
Market Penetration	Perception	Existing Products, Existing Markets	Leaders utilize perception to deepen market share by understanding customer needs and competitive landscapes, optimizing strategies, and fostering loyalty.
Product Development	Wisdom	New Products, Existing Markets	Wisdom drives innovation to create new products for current audiences, ensuring alignment with market demands and enhancing product lines.

Quadrant	Attribute	Focus	Description
Market Development	Wisdom and Perception	Existing Products, New Markets	Wisdom evaluates market readiness, while perception adapts products to new contexts, addressing barriers and opportunities in market expansion.
Diversification	Intuition	New Products, New Markets	Intuition navigates unfamiliar territory, anticipating trends and risks. This quadrant demands bold innovation, risk-taking, and visionary leadership.

Each quadrant of the Growth Matrix connects with the Ajna Chakra's attributes, providing a clearer path for leaders to channel these energies into strategies for conscious growth.

Energetic Takeaways: Ajna

1. Intuitive Energy: Ajna encourages foresight and intuition, enabling leaders to make informed decisions even in uncertain situations.
2. Visionary Energy: This energy supports the ability to visualize long-term goals and strategize effectively.
3. Perceptive Energy: Ajna fosters clarity of thought, enhancing the ability to analyze complex situations and identify solutions.

The Ajna Matrix demonstrates the interaction between balanced and unbalanced energies of foresight and vision, offering a framework for strategic thinking and clarity in leadership.

Ajna Matrix
Balanced Energy

Sahasrara
(The Crown Chakra)

Sahasrara (*suh-hah-srur-uh*) means "thousand-petaled." At first glance, the Sahasrara, or Crown Chakra, may seem rooted in religious ideals, but it transcends traditional theistic interpretations. Located at the top of the head, it is symbolized by a radiant lotus with a thousand petals, representing spiritual enlightenment, higher consciousness, and universal connection. This Chakra extends beyond the physical self, fostering a connection to Divine or Universal wisdom and a profound sense of unity with all beings. In Yogic culture, this idea is beautifully conveyed through the concept of "Vasudhaiva Kutumbakam," meaning the world is one family.

An energized Crown Chakra brings clarity, peace, and a sense of connection to a purpose beyond personal ambition. Leaders with an open Sahasrara focus on purpose-driven goals and impact rather than numerical success. This heightened awareness enables them to transcend transactional relationships, leading with wisdom and a vision of unity and higher order.

The Sahasrara encompasses numerous qualities, many of which may seem abstract, but they can be distilled into two essential attributes: Enlightenment and Transcendence:

Enlightenment

Enlightenment, at its core, is the state of attaining deep understanding, clarity, and wisdom beyond ordinary perception. In spiritual traditions, it is often regarded as the pinnacle of human consciousness—a transcendent insight into the true nature of reality. Buddha's journey to enlightenment under the Bodhi tree stands as one of history's most profound examples. Through intense meditation and self-reflection, he reached a state of ultimate wisdom, free from suffering, inspiring countless individuals to pursue similar clarity in their own lives.

In a contemporary business context, enlightenment takes a more pragmatic form. Often referred to as a 'paradigm shift,' it describes a leader's awakening to a deeper purpose, typically sparked by personal reflection, awareness of social or environmental impacts, or life-altering experiences. This enlightenment prompts business leaders to rethink not only what they do but why they do it, guiding themselves or their organizations toward more conscientious and meaningful directions.

In *The Enlightened Capitalists*, James O'Toole explores how visionary business leaders balance profitability with positive societal impact, embodying the essence of enlightenment in the corporate world. O'Toole highlights leaders who experience transformative shifts, realizing that business success can coexist with responsibility. For example, Paul Polman, as CEO of Unilever, launched the "Sustainable Living Plan," placing social and environmental impact above short-term financial gain. Similarly, Larry Fink of BlackRock emphasized purpose alongside profits, advocating for corporations to adopt environmental, social, and governance (ESG) principles.

The Crown Chakra's concept of enlightenment aligns closely with *Servant Leadership*, a model introduced by Robert Greenleaf. Enlightened leaders rise above self-interest, prioritizing the growth and well-being of others. They lead with humility, focusing on uplifting their teams rather than asserting dominance. This approach embodies a higher state of consciousness, where true power lies in service and compassion. Enlightenment in business often involves the wisdom to discern what not to pursue. Leaders with an enlightened vision recognize when to pivot, abandon harmful practices, and embrace new, purposeful paths.

Transcendence

Transcendence, in its philosophical essence, involves rising above the ego, personal ambitions, and immediate interests to connect with a broader, universal consciousness. It is about elevating one's perspective to align with a higher purpose. The *Bhagavad Gita* encapsulates this idea in Krishna's words: *"When a man lets go of all desires of his heart and is satisfied within himself, then he is said to be one with the divine."*

Transcendence requires a profound shift in consciousness, which is only possible when the Sahasrara Chakra is fully activated and balanced. Dr. A.P.J. Abdul Kalam, former President of India and a renowned scientist, delves into this concept in *Transcendence*. In his reflections, Dr. Kalam discusses how the integration of science and spirituality can elevate human potential, fostering a deeper sense of purpose and clarity. He highlights that transcendence is not merely an abstract idea, but a practical and transformative state that enables individuals to connect with a larger purpose beyond personal limitations. This elevated consciousness empowers leaders to move beyond the ego, inspiring creativity, resilience, and fulfillment. By embracing a higher vision, leaders can not only align their own goals with a greater purpose, but also inspire collective growth and innovation.

While transcendence is often linked to spiritual or religious practices, it is a universal experience that transcends specific beliefs. It represents a heightened state of awareness—a natural "high" requiring no external substances, offering euphoria and clarity that empowers individuals to overcome challenges. For leaders, transcendence provides an opportunity to step back from daily pressures, fostering a broader perspective that enhances their potential and impact within the organization and beyond. As Dr. Kalam emphasizes, transcendence through meditation and mindfulness practices allows leaders to achieve this state naturally and sustainably, enabling them to lead with insight, patience, and compassion.

For many accomplished individuals, transcendental meditation (TM) and practices like Vipassana meditation have been pivotal in achieving transcendence. Ray Dalio, founder of Bridgewater Associates, credits TM as the single most influential factor in his personal and professional success, stating, "Meditation more than anything in my life was the biggest ingredient of whatever success I've had." Similarly, historian and author Yuval Noah Harari emphasizes the impact of Vipassana on his ability to gain profound insights into human behavior and history. Harari notes that meditation provides the clarity and focus needed to cut through the noise of the present, enabling him to connect with timeless truths.

In Maslow's Hierarchy of Needs, self-actualization represents the pinnacle of human potential, where individuals pursue purposes beyond themselves. This concept aligns with the energy of the Crown Chakra, which inspires transcendence of ego and commitment to a higher purpose. Abraham Maslow described self-actualized leaders as driven by creativity, ethics, and a desire to leave a positive legacy. Similarly, Daniel Pink, in *Drive*, highlights that autonomy, mastery, and purpose—qualities linked to the Sahasrara Chakra—are powerful workplace motivators, showing that individuals often seek growth, meaning, and contributions beyond financial rewards.

Conscious capitalism emerges as a compelling alternative to the inherent shortcomings of socialism and leftist ideologies. I advocate capitalism as a driver of human progress, innovation, and individual empowerment, in contrast to socialism and leftism, which often falter under their own contradictions. Leftist ideals, while cloaked in lofty rhetoric, frequently prove elitist and disconnected from the realities of everyday people. Margaret Thatcher's observation remains relevant: "The problem with socialism is you eventually run out of other people's money."

For business leaders, moving beyond a narrow focus on immediate gains or personal agendas unlocks a broader perspective centered on purpose, integrity, and societal impact. This transcendence enhances individual performance, inspires trust, motivates teams, and aligns everyone with the organization's core mission. Ultimately, it becomes a transformative force that shapes not only the character of a leader but also the values and purpose of the organization.

———

Energetic Takeaways: Sahasrara

1. Integrative Energy: Sahasrara symbolizes the integration of knowledge and wisdom, encouraging holistic decision-making in business.
2. Transformative Energy: This energy fosters a connection to higher purpose, driving innovation and meaningful impact.
3. Enlightening Energy: Sahasrara inspires a vision beyond immediate goals, cultivating a culture of mindfulness and long-term growth.

The Sahasrara Matrix explores the balance and imbalance in wisdom and purpose, offering a pathway to align decisions and actions with a higher purpose for meaningful impact.

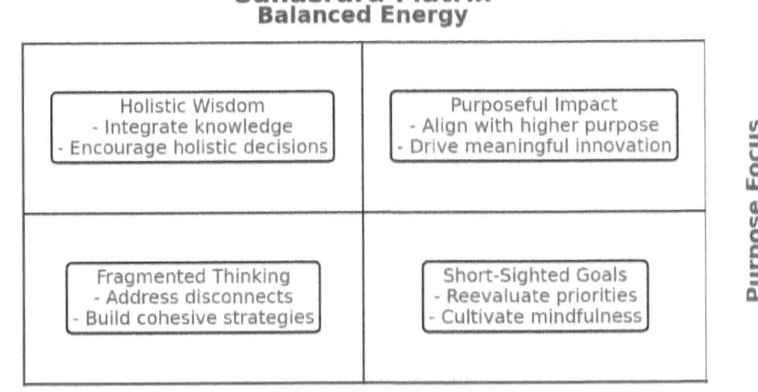

The exploration of the seven chakras uncovers their powerful application in business, offering a framework to understand energy flow in individuals and organizations. Connecting chakra attributes with business practices provides a holistic approach, enhancing resilience, creativity, and strategic insight. Balanced chakras ensure the seamless flow of Prana, sustaining vitality and awareness. For leaders, this understanding offers a new perspective on organizational dynamics and personal growth. Far from being abstract symbols, the chakras serve as practical tools for optimizing individual and collective potential.

Up next, we explore Ida and Pingala to further understand this system's dual energy balance.

Ida and Pingala

The concepts of Ida and Pingala Nadi also originate from ancient yogic traditions, representing the dual flows of energy within the human system. Drawing on the teachings of Sadhguru and ancient texts, Ida and Pingala are understood as the two primary energy channels that intertwine along the spine, flanking the central Sushumna Nadi. These energies are often compared to the solar and lunar currents in the body, symbolizing a balance between contrasting yet complementary forces.

- Ida is associated with the left side of the body and the right hemisphere of the brain. Connected to the Chandra Nadi (Lunar Energy), it governs cooling, calming, and introspective aspects. Ida is linked to the parasympathetic nervous system, responsible for the "rest and digest" functions of the body. It fosters relaxation, reflection, and creative thinking—attributes closely aligned with strategic planning in a business context.

- Pingala is connected to the right side of the body and the left hemisphere of the brain. It corresponds to the Surya Nadi (Solar Energy), symbolizing heat, action, and dynamism. Pingala influences the sympathetic nervous system, which drives the "fight or flight" response. It embodies action, focus, and execution—qualities essential for operations and daily business activities.

Sadhguru eloquently compares these channels to the two wings of a bird. For a bird to soar high, both wings must work in harmony. Similarly, in business, strategic thinking (Ida) and operational execution (Pingala) must function together to achieve sustainable growth. Just as a bird requires balance, businesses must maintain a dynamic equilibrium between introspective planning and decisive action.

Peter Drucker, the pioneer of modern management, highlighted the significance of strategic thinking with his statement: "Management is doing things right; leadership is doing the right things." This emphasizes the need for leaders to harness the cooling, reflective energy of Ida, ensuring their strategies align with the broader vision of the organization.

The Ida and Pingala energies closely parallel the roles of the sympathetic and parasympathetic nervous systems in the human body. The sympathetic nervous system, which activates the fight-or-flight response in high-stress situations, aligns with Pingala energy—focused, action-oriented, and decisive. This energy serves as the operational engine of a business, enabling swift execution and immediate results when required.

On the other hand, the parasympathetic nervous system, responsible for "rest and digest," parallels Ida energy, which nurtures creativity, introspection, and strategic thinking. Just as the parasympathetic system facilitates recovery and renewal, businesses thrive when they dedicate time to brainstorming, off-site retreats, and reflective moments. The phrase "take a step back" underscores this need—pausing the daily grind to reassess, recalibrate, and reconnect with the bigger picture.

The Myth of Long Working Hours

Modern work culture, particularly in Asian countries, often glorifies long hours and constant busyness as markers of productivity. Some successful entrepreneurs even advocate for 72-hour work weeks. However, this mindset neglects the importance of balanced energy flow—between Ida and Pingala, rest and action, strategy and execution. Eric Jorgensen, in *The Almanack of Naval Ravikant*, wisely observes, "Play long-term games with long-term people. But remember, time spent well is more valuable than time spent long." This highlights that effectiveness is determined not by the quantity of hours worked but by the quality and intention behind them.

In *The 4-Hour Work Week*, Tim Ferriss challenges the conventional 40-hour work week, asserting that most tasks can be completed far more efficiently with focus and intentionality. He introduces the concept of the "minimum effective dose," encouraging the elimination of trivial tasks to concentrate on high-impact activities. This principle mirrors the balance of Ida and Pingala energies—fostering deep, strategic thinking without overextending into excessive action. While I find it difficult to imagine achieving meaningful results in under an hour a day, the phrase likely serves as a metaphor rather than a literal suggestion. Regardless, the book is both engaging and thought-provoking.

Ferriss's perspective highlights a key insight often overlooked in business: shorter, more focused work hours can yield better results than rigid, long-hour schedules. This method not only mitigates burnout but also aligns with the principles of optimizing energy flow. Just as the body alternates between sympathetic and parasympathetic states, businesses thrive by balancing periods of intense activity with moments of rest and reflection.

Strategic Reflection vs. Operational Execution

Henry Mintzberg, in *The Rise and Fall of Strategic Planning*, underscores the importance of integrating strategy and execution. He argues that strategy must remain flexible, evolving through a cycle of action and reflection—mirroring the dynamic interplay of Ida and Pingala. Leaders must continuously adapt their strategies based on real-time feedback from execution efforts, ensuring a harmonious approach.

Strategy and operations are often viewed as separate, rigid entities. However, true effectiveness stems from their interconnectedness, much like the intertwining of Ida and Pingala Nadis. Strategy (Ida) provides creative vision and long-term direction, while operations (Pingala) ensures precise and efficient execution. As Jepser Jorensen at Stanford says, a strategy is an argument for how an organization creates and captures value, and to be meaningful, it must be based on a set of assumptions about a future that is at least partially knowable, but testable! Without balancing these energies, a company risks stagnation, where excess Ida leads to a lack of action, or burnout, where excess Pingala results in a lack of reflection.

The concept of Ambidextrous Leadership emphasizes this balance, calling for leaders to integrate exploration (intuition/strategy) with exploitation (execution/action). In *Lead and Disrupt*, Michael Tushman and Charles O'Reilly illustrate how ambidextrous organizations succeed by balancing innovation (Ida) with operational efficiency (Pingala). This duality enables businesses to explore new opportunities while maintaining the core functions that drive immediate results.

The Futility of Defined Working Hours

For roles requiring creative thinking, problem-solving, or strategic planning, rigid working hours often prove counterproductive. While assembly-line tasks may demand fixed schedules, modern business roles thrive on flexibility, which boosts productivity and innovation. This approach mirrors the flow of pranic energy, allowing cycles of reflection (Ida) and execution (Pingala) to remain balanced.

The growing trend of flexible working hours and remote work reflects an understanding of the limitations of traditional, rigid schedules. By giving employees the freedom to align their work with their natural energy patterns, businesses can unlock greater creativity and efficiency, much like the balanced flow of Ida and Pingala energies.

That said, I firmly believe balance is essential. Work-from-office setups play a critical role in fostering a strong organizational culture—a business's greatest competitive advantage. While remote work offers flexibility, it risks diluting the sense of belonging, collaboration, and shared purpose that office environments naturally cultivate. A purely remote approach can lead to isolation and weaken the creation of a unique work culture that drives long-term success.

Ultimately, businesses must strike a balance between flexibility and structure. By blending the autonomy of remote work with the synergy of in-person collaboration, organizations can nurture both individual productivity and a vibrant, cohesive culture.

———

Energetic Takeaways: Ida and Pingala

1. ntuitive Energy (Ida): Represents creativity, introspection, and emotional intelligence, guiding strategic decisions through intuition.

2. Logical Energy (Pingala): Embodies structure, execution, and analytical thinking, driving efficient operations and results.

3. Dynamic Balance: Ida and Pingala together symbolize the harmony of intuition and logic, ensuring both strategic vision and practical execution.

4. Organizational Flow: The balance between these energies fosters a seamless workflow, enhancing adaptability and innovation.

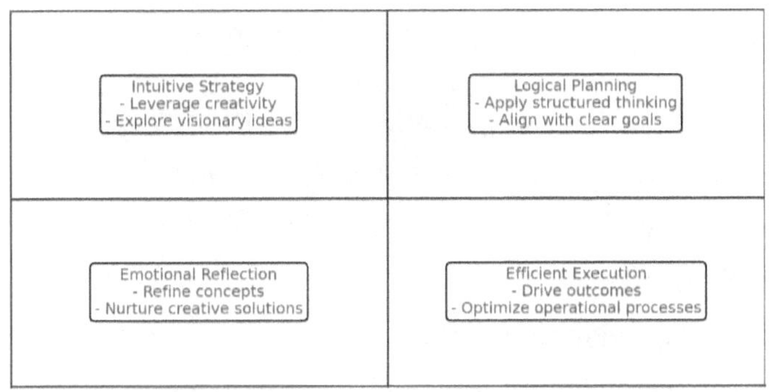

How Do We Achieve Balance in the Seven Chakras and Ida and Pingala?

Energising and balancing the seven chakras alongside the channels of Ida and Pingala may seem challenging at first glance, yet it is remarkably achievable with awareness and intent. The ancient science of yoga offers profound, time-tested methods to harmonize these energetic centers and channels.

This balance begins with understanding that each chakra and energy channel plays a unique role in shaping our physical, mental, and spiritual well-being. By drawing from ancient wisdom and adopting Yogic principles, we can create harmony within ourselves and extend this equilibrium to our professional endeavors.

In the context of business, the interplay of Ida and Pingala channels serves as a metaphor for the balance between strategic reflection and operational execution. Just as these channels complement each other to foster inner harmony, businesses thrive when planning and execution work in unison, creating a dynamic yet balanced approach to growth and success.

In the following sections, we will explore these timeless principles, uncovering practical ways to foster balance within ourselves and our organizations. By aligning with these teachings, we unlock our fullest potential and cultivate an enduring foundation for both personal and professional excellence.

PART THREE

The HOW.

"Whatever kind of business you are into, ultimately, there is only one business—that is human wellbeing."

– Sadhguru

Ashtanga Yoga:
The Eight Limbs of Yoga

The timeless principles of yoga provide a guiding framework for understanding its true purpose, especially in today's increasingly interconnected, volatile, uncertain, complex, and ambiguous - VUCA - world. As discussed earlier in this book, energizing the seven chakras and balancing the channels of Ida and Pingala are essential for fostering harmony in both personal and professional aspects of life. Yet, this task can seem daunting—how do we achieve balance and elevate consciousness while navigating the relentless pace and demands of modern life?

The answer lies in the comprehensive and enduring philosophy of Yoga, which extends far beyond physical fitness to serve as a pathway to holistic well-being and higher consciousness. While often associated with asanas (physical postures), yoga's true essence is much deeper, as outlined in the *Yoga Sutras* by Patanjali, the ancient sage who formalized its teachings. These teachings are encapsulated in the eightfold path known as Ashtanga Yoga, providing practical steps to achieve balance, clarity, and purpose in a complex world.

What is Ashtanga Yoga?

Ashtanga (*ush-taan-guh*), or the Eight Limbs of Yoga, was introduced by Patanjali as a structured path to self-realization and spiritual growth. Often mistaken as a distinct style of yoga, Ashtanga represents the comprehensive framework underlying all yoga practices. It encompasses eight interconnected limbs that work together to cultivate harmony in life, emphasizing that each limb is an integral part of the whole.

This practice, however, is not limited to personal development; it is crucial for the leadership of any organization to embody these principles in their personal lives. Leadership is most effective when it leads by example—practicing values such as integrity, mindfulness, and balance in day-to-day decisions. As the saying goes, "You cannot compartmentalize character." There is no such thing as being a good person and a bad businessperson—or vice versa. Leadership that integrates personal ethics with professional responsibilities sets a standard that inspires teams, shapes organizational culture, and drives sustainable success.

The Eight Limbs of Yoga are:

1. Yama (the principles),
2. Niyama (the discipline),

3. Asana (the actions),
4. Pranayama (the control),
5. Pratyahara (the withdrawal)
6. Dharana (the absorption),
7. Dhyana (the focus), and
8. Samadhi (the actualization).

The sequence of these limbs is vital because each builds upon the previous one, forming an integrated approach to life. They are not isolated steps but interconnected principles, much like the relationship between strategy and execution or intuition and logic in business. Just as in business, where strategy is meaningless without effective execution, no limb of yoga can function independently of the others.

A Higher Purpose

We often think of business as a separate domain from personal life, driven by goals, competition, and outcomes. However, when we look deeper, business, like yoga, serves a higher purpose. As Sadhguru aptly observes, the ultimate aim of any activity—be it business or otherwise—is human well-being. Tragically, even destructive actions like war often stem from a misguided interpretation of serving one's people or ensuring their well-being.

The paradox, often referred to as the Paradox of Benevolence, arises when the pursuit of well-being for some leads to harm for others—a result of limited consciousness and self-awareness. For instance, a dictator may justify waging war as a means to improve life for his people, ignoring the far-reaching consequences. Similarly, business leaders may prioritize profit-driven decisions that benefit shareholders in the short term but ultimately harm communities, employees, or the environment—systems that the shareholders themselves depend on for long-term stability and prosperity.

This is where the Eight Limbs of Yoga become invaluable—not only for transforming personal consciousness but also for shaping ethical, balanced, and mindful business practices while staying true to the mission of benevolence. By integrating the principles of Ashtanga Yoga into business, leaders can harmonize the seven chakras and the two energy channels, aligning their goals with the broader well-being of society. This approach ensures that their actions are guided by ethics, discipline, focus, and compassion, all while maintaining profitability and driving wealth creation.

Let's explore each limb of Yoga:

Yama
(The Principles)

We are our thoughts. Our face, often described as the index of our thoughts, reflects our inner world. Thoughts shape actions, actions form habits, habits build character, and character defines our aura. While the concept of aura might seem esoteric to some, it is both a physical and metaphysical phenomenon.

On a physical level, aura is an electrical corona discharge emanating from the body, which can be visualized using Kirlian photography. On a metaphysical level, it represents the vibrational frequency we emit—our energy signature—that can attract or repel others without a word being exchanged.

As our aura influences what and who we draw into our lives, it becomes a determinant of our destiny. After all, is it not what or who we attract or repel a critical factor shaping the course of our lives?

Principles are the distilled essence of our highest thoughts. At their core, every principle originates as a thought—a mental seed that, through reflection and repetition, evolves into a guiding value or belief. In this way, thoughts serve as the raw material from which principles are forged. Conversely, once established, principles function as a compass, shaping and refining our thoughts. They become a reference point, guiding the kinds of thoughts we permit ourselves to nurture and act upon.

In the context of business, principles or core values are foundational. They emerge from the collective thoughts of a company's founders and leaders. However, research indicates that many organizations lack a formal mission statement. Even among those that do, these statements often remain superficial, serving as decorative elements rather than true guiding principles. A study by Achievers revealed that 61 percent of employees are unaware of their company's mission statement, and 57 percent are not motivated by it. This highlights the adage, "If you do not know where you are going, any road will take you there."

While mission statements may seem overused in management discussions, they remain fundamental to an organization's direction and purpose. Just as every modern construction, no matter how advanced, still requires a solid foundation, distilling thoughts into principles or Yamas is essential, as they inevitably manifest into reality over time.

There are five Yamas in Yogic philosophy that form the ethical foundation of our thoughts. Let us explore each of them in the context of today's interconnected and dynamic world:

Ahimsa (Non-Violence)

Ahimsa, often understood as non-violence, encompasses much more than refraining from physical harm. It also involves avoiding emotional, verbal, and psychological harm to others. In a business context, Ahimsa inspires leadership rooted in empathy, respect, and compassion, fostering a culture where people feel valued and supported.

A modern embodiment of the principle of Ahimsa in business is social compliance. At its core, social compliance involves adhering to the laws of the land in which a business operates, as no law is inherently designed to harm its people. The variation lies in the implementation and enforcement across different countries.

A key private organization championing social compliance is London-based Sedex, where I had the privilege of serving on the board for six years. Sedex facilitates responsible supply chains and comprises thousands of member organizations globally, each committed to upholding social compliance as responsible businesses. By promoting ethical labor practices, fair wages, and safe working conditions, social compliance reflects the essence of Ahimsa, fostering respect, compassion, and non-violence in the business world.

In practical terms, businesses that practice Ahimsa foster cultures of inclusivity, diversity, and psychological safety, where employees feel respected, valued, and free from emotional harm. Such organizations reject workplace bullying, toxic competition, and unethical behavior. They also ensure that their products, services, and operations avoid causing harm to people or the environment, reflecting a commitment to non-violence in every aspect of their practices.

Google conducted an internal study, "Project Aristotle," which revealed psychological safety as the most critical factor in building successful and innovative teams. This principle fosters an environment where employees feel safe to voice their ideas, share concerns, and express themselves without fear of retribution or embarrassment. By prioritizing psychological safety, Google has successfully driven innovation and enhanced collaboration across the organization.

Satya (Truthfulness)

Satya extends beyond simply speaking the truth; it involves perceiving reality with clarity and aligning actions with that truth. Rooted in an energized Vishuddha (Throat Chakra), Satya enables leaders to cultivate transparency and authenticity—essential elements for building trust and accountability. Leaders who embody Satya foster open and honest communication with employees, customers, and shareholders, ensuring that integrity becomes a cornerstone of their organizational culture.

A common practice among companies embracing Satya is organizing Town Halls or conducting anonymous employee surveys to promote open dialogue and transparency. These initiatives enable leadership to share updates, discuss challenges, and communicate performance, while providing employees a platform to offer feedback and ask questions. Such practices foster trust, reinforce accountability, and ensure the company remains aligned with its core values.

Bridgewater Associates exemplifies Satya through its culture of radical transparency, encouraging open dialogue and clear decision-making. Similarly, Everlane reflects this principle by openly sharing its pricing structure and ethical sourcing, fostering trust with its customers.

Satya rejects half-truths, emphasizing complete honesty in all actions and communications. Deceptive marketing may yield short-term gains, but as the old adage reminds us, "You can fool some of the people all the time and all the people some of the time, but you cannot fool all the people all the time." The truth ultimately surfaces and prevails. The collapse of the American meat company Belcampo, which falsely labeled its products as sustainably sourced, is just one example of the inevitable consequences of dishonesty.

Sometimes, legislation plays a crucial role in letting *Satya* prevail. A notable example is the Digital Product Passport (DPP), introduced under the EU's Ecodesign for Sustainable Products Regulation (ESPR), which came into effect in 2024. The DPP is set to become mandatory between 2026 and 2030, starting with industries like textiles, electronics, and batteries. This initiative will provide comprehensive, digital records of a product's lifecycle, including details on materials, sourcing, environmental impact, and end-of-life disposal. By enabling consumers and businesses to make informed, ethical choices, the DPP fosters accountability and transparency across supply chains. This is a significant step toward embedding truthfulness and trustworthiness into global business practices.

In short, Satya in business is about creating a culture of openness and integrity, where truthfulness is embedded in both internal operations and external engagements.

Asteya (Non-Stealing)

Asteya (*us-teya*), often translated as non-stealing, extends far beyond the act of refraining from theft. It embodies the principle of giving back in proportion to what one takes—be it from individuals, nature, or communities. This concept applies not only to tangible resources but also to intangible elements such as credit, respect, and appreciation.

The concepts of carbon neutrality and net-zero emissions exemplify Asteya in action. Carbon neutrality involves balancing the amount of carbon dioxide emitted with an equivalent offset, such as tree planting or purchasing carbon credits. Net-zero, however, takes this further by focusing on reducing emissions as much as possible across all operations and value chains without relying on carbon credits. These goals are essential for businesses dedicated to sustainability.

Companies like Interface, a leader in modular flooring, have achieved carbon neutrality through innovative recycling practices and renewable energy adoption. Similarly, companies such as Colgate-Palmolive are actively working toward net-zero emissions, demonstrating a commitment to reducing their environmental footprint and giving back in proportion to what they take.

Just compensation and ethical reciprocity align closely with the principles of Asteya. Businesses practicing Asteya ensure fair treatment and pay for their employees while prioritizing sustainable practices that protect natural resources and support local communities.

The Fair Trade system, established in 1997 and headquartered in Bonn, Germany, is a notable embodiment of Asteya. It promotes ethical production practices, ensuring that farmers and factory workers, even at the base of the supply chain, receive fair wages and work in safe conditions, fostering equity and sustainability in global trade.

The Amsterdam-based Fair Wear Foundation has played a pivotal role in securing fair wages and improving working conditions for millions of garment workers. Similarly, the Circular Economy Alliance, a global leader in training and certification, has advanced the practical application of circular economy principles, equipping individuals and organizations to champion sustainable change.

Businesses embracing circular economy practices aim to minimize waste by reusing and recycling materials, ensuring resources are responsibly reintegrated into the system. This approach reflects the principles of Asteya, fostering sustainability and mitigating the depletion of natural resources.

Recycled polyester, derived from PET bottles, and recycled cotton yarn, created from post-consumer clothing, are revolutionizing waste management and advancing sustainability in the fashion industry. Recycled polyester prevents millions of plastic bottles from polluting oceans and landfills, reducing environmental impact, lowering carbon emissions, and supporting a circular economy. Similarly, recycled cotton yarn breathes new life into discarded textiles, diminishing the demand for virgin cotton, conserving water, and shrinking the garment industry's environmental footprint. Together, these innovations showcase sustainable practices that tackle critical global challenges.

Kariban Brands embodies Asteya by prioritizing ethical production, ensuring fair wages, and adopting sustainable practices. The company champions safe working conditions and incorporates eco-friendly materials, such as organic and recycled cotton, demonstrating its commitment to both environmental and social responsibility.

TOMS Shoes offers another compelling example of Asteya in action. Through its one-for-one model, TOMS donates a product to someone in need for every product sold. This reciprocal approach exemplifies the principle of giving back in proportion to what is taken, creating a meaningful societal impact.

Asteya extends to intellectual property, underscoring the importance of respecting the work and ideas of others. Ethical collaboration, marked by proper recognition and fair credit, embodies the principle of non-stealing in the realms of innovation and knowledge sharing. In writing this book, I have drawn from the rich reservoir of ancient wisdom and modern management literature, incorporating insights and referencing them in the bibliography. If any credit has been inadvertently omitted, I humbly seek forgiveness, as honoring the principle of Asteya is my sincere intent.

Aparigraha (Non-Possessiveness)

Aparigraha (*a-pa-ri-gra-ha*), or non-possessiveness, is a fundamental Yama and a cornerstone of Yogic living. It advocates owning only what is necessary and releasing excess for the greater good. This principle challenges the human tendency to cling to material possessions, often at the expense of deeper fulfillment. Yogic philosophy teaches that "those with the ability to do good have a responsibility to do so, lest the Universe reallocate those abilities." This profound wisdom reminds us that material things are impermanent, and excessive attachment to them can diminish our joy, purpose, and capacity to contribute meaningfully to society.

Being "possessed by possessions" is not only harmful to the individual but also detrimental to society. Philanthropy, regardless of its material size, plays a vital role in bridging the gap between the haves and have-nots, fostering societal harmony and progress. Even those without material wealth can contribute by sharing their time or knowledge to make a meaningful impact. As Andrew Carnegie wisely stated, "Surplus wealth is a sacred trust which its possessor is bound to administer in his lifetime for the good of the community."

For individuals and businesses alike, practicing Aparigraha involves channeling surplus resources—whether cash, assets, or knowledge—toward societal initiatives, business growth, or dividends to create shared value. Neglecting this responsibility risks societal disintegration, underscoring the importance of letting go for the greater collective good.

The principles in Joshua Becker's *The Minimalist Home* reflect the essence of Aparigraha. Becker emphasizes simplifying our surroundings to foster intentionality and fulfillment. In a business context, this philosophy translates to adopting minimalist practices—eliminating excess and focusing on what truly matters. A common barrier to letting go of possessions is the reluctance to discard functional items. Repurposing offers a meaningful solution. Organizations like Goonj in India and the Salvation Army in the UK specialize in repurposing surplus goods, providing for those in need while generating the positive energy and clarity that come from decluttering.

One effective strategy for decluttering is to reduce storage space. Homes without lofts, attics, or garages naturally remain free from excessive accumulation. Similarly, offices with minimalist furniture, such as desks without drawers, encourage cleanliness and radiate positive energy. Yet, many of us struggle to part with unnecessary items—like briefcases carried for months or years, filled with scraps of paper that serve no purpose.

Apple Stores exemplify this principle in their retail design, eliminating traditional checkout counters altogether. By empowering every employee to act as a cashier, their sleek, minimalist approach not only reflects Aparigraha but also enhances the customer experience, proving that less can indeed be more.

In the software industry, agile development embodies the philosophy of Aparigraha by prioritizing essential features, iterative improvements, and streamlined processes. Similarly, lean management focuses on eliminating waste to enhance efficiency and create value. In contrast, businesses that cling to obsolete inventory or office clutter—often justified by perceived future utility or balance sheet considerations—end up tying up valuable capital and wasting resources. Aparigraha teaches that letting go of excess, whether physical or strategic, fosters clarity, productivity, and sustainable growth.

The philanthropic efforts of Bob and Dottie King illustrate that charity goes beyond aiding the disempowered; it can also nurture potential and foster growth when applied thoughtfully. Embracing the principle of non-possessiveness, the Kings established the Stanford Seed Transformation Program, an innovative initiative that empowers small and medium-sized enterprises (SMEs) in economically challenged regions. Rather than holding onto their wealth, they chose to invest it in driving economic growth and fostering innovation. Their generosity embodies the essence of Aparigraha, demonstrating how purposeful giving can create sustainable impact and lasting change.

In stark contrast, much of Africa—a continent richly endowed with natural resources—remains impoverished due to the hoarding of wealth by corrupt dictators. Leaders like Sani Abacha of Nigeria and Mobutu Sese Seko of the Democratic Republic of the Congo (DRC) siphoned billions of dollars into secret offshore accounts, depriving their nations of critical development resources. In 2014, the U.S. Department of Justice successfully forfeited $480 million of Abacha's assets, marking the largest kleptocracy forfeiture ever achieved. Similarly, in 1988, a Belgian court ordered the seizure of several properties owned by Mobutu in Belgium. These actions represent only a fraction of the widespread corruption that has perpetuated cycles of poverty and underdevelopment in regions abundant in natural resources.

Closer to home in India, certain political families have amassed vast fortunes through questionable means. Ironically, the wealth accumulated by such corrupt individuals often remains unusable, as they must maintain the facade of poverty. This paradox highlights the futility of excessive accumulation—proving that even immense riches fail to bring fulfillment or freedom when cloaked in secrecy and pretense.

Unchecked personal indulgences often become symbols of possessiveness. Ramalinga Raju of Satyam initially garnered sympathy for confessing to accounting fraud, but this quickly faded when investigators revealed his collection of thousands of designer suits. Similarly, Imelda Marcos, the former First Lady of the Philippines, remains infamous for her collection of over a thousand pairs of luxury shoes, highlighting the glaring contrast between her lavish lifestyle and the widespread poverty endured by her country.

The art world provides another striking example, where priceless artworks are hidden away in freeports in locations like Geneva, Luxembourg, and Singapore. These duty-free storage facilities allow the wealthy to hoard valuable art as investment assets that would never be seen by the public—contradicting the very purpose for which the artist created the piece. This practice stands in stark contrast to the principle of Aparigraha.

Wealth finds its true worth not in mere accumulation, but in how it is put to use. Even if not used for philanthropy, responsible consumption leads to a good greater than possession. That is why I believe the lavish Ambani wedding of 2024, with nearly a billion dollars spent, was justified. Although some criticized it as a display of extravagance, the event undoubtedly generated employment and provided economic benefits, benefitting countless individuals in the process, not to mention the $10 billion brand that the Ambani's might have built up in the process.

Brahmacharya (Continence/Moderation)

Brahmacharya (*bruh-hum-cha-urya*), often translated as continence, is more accurately understood as the practice of moderation and self-restraint. It encourages balance in our actions, steering clear of both indulgence and deprivation. This principle intersects with the Yamas of Asteya (non-stealing) and Aparigraha (non-possessiveness), emphasizing that no Yogic philosophy stands alone. Each principle complements the others, forming a balanced and holistic approach to life and leadership. In yoga, nothing is rigidly absolute; instead, it is a continual effort to harmonize various aspects of thought and behavior.

Expanding its meaning further, Brahmacharya does not advocate abstinence within a committed relationship but emphasizes fidelity and focus within that bond. Few things drain energy—emotional, mental, physical, or financial—as profoundly as pursuing relationships outside the one to which we are committed. While such relationships may appear alluring, offering a fleeting sense of excitement or fulfillment, they often, like nectar turning to poison, result in broken trust, emotional turmoil, and financial strain.

Esther Perel, in her book *The State of Affairs: Rethinking Infidelity*, explores the complexities of such relationships, shedding light on how they disrupt personal balance and create unintended consequences. The distractions and emotional toll of these entanglements often spill over into professional life, diminishing focus, impairing decision-making, and reducing overall effectiveness. Brahmacharya serves as a reminder that disciplined focus and balance are essential, not just in personal relationships, but also in maintaining integrity in professional roles.

Leaders who embody Brahmacharya recognize that fidelity and moderation are not merely moral virtues but essential tools for preserving energy, maintaining clarity, and sustaining focus. History is replete with cautionary tales of individuals whose personal indiscretions led to professional downfalls. While specifics may not be necessary, such examples illustrate how distractions can cause reputational damage, undermine trust, and even unravel entire organizations. A lack of personal discipline often seeps into professional conduct, eroding credibility, alienating teams, and tarnishing legacies. These instances underscore the essence of Brahmacharya: moderation and restraint are indispensable for both personal and professional longevity.

Practicing Brahmacharya helps channel energy toward what truly matters—building enduring relationships, fostering trust, and driving sustainable value. It also highlights the importance of ethical decision-making and prudent resource management. Leaders embracing this principle ensure their companies avoid overextension in the relentless pursuit of short-term gains, instead prioritizing long-term success. By managing resources wisely and ethically, they strike a balance between ambition and responsibility. This approach cultivates a culture of integrity, prevents organizational burnout, and strengthens trust with teams and stakeholders, creating a legacy of lasting impact.

Yogic Takeaways

1. The Power of Principles
   - Our thoughts shape our actions, habits, and ultimately our destiny. Core principles, when rooted in clarity and intent, serve as a guiding compass for both individuals and organizations.
2. Ahimsa (Non-Violence)
   - Ahimsa extends beyond physical harm to encompass emotional, verbal, and psychological safety. Businesses that prioritize inclusivity, diversity, and ethical practices foster trust and innovation.
3. Satya (Truthfulness)
   - Satya involves clarity, honesty, and transparency in both actions and communications. Half-truths may bring short-term gains but lead to long-term consequences, as truth always prevails.
4. Asteya (Non-Stealing)
   - Asteya is about giving back proportionately to what is taken—be it tangible resources or intangible elements like credit and respect. Ethical production, fair trade, and sustainability are modern manifestations of Asteya.
5. Aparigraha (Non-Possessiveness)
   - Aparigraha calls for letting go of excess and using wealth responsibly for collective benefit. Minimalism, philanthropy, and responsible consumption embody this principle.

6. Brahmacharya (Moderation)

- Brahmacharya is self-restraint and disciplined focus. Leaders practicing Brahmacharya avoid indulgence and channel their energy into meaningful pursuits, fostering sustainable growth and trust.

Niyama (The Discipline)

While Yama governs our relationship with the external world, Niyama shifts the focus inward, emphasizing internal discipline and our relationship with ourselves. These principles foster self-regulation, self-awareness, and personal integrity. Niyama serves as the foundation for sustained growth, guiding the cultivation of habits essential for long-term resilience and success.

True discipline in business is not about making bold, attention-grabbing statements but about consistency and follow-through. It is the ability to persist even when motivation wanes, ensuring that efforts lead to lasting success. Many businesses launch initiatives with great enthusiasm, but without the discipline to sustain focus, these efforts often lack depth and long-term impact.

Niyama cultivates resilience, personal growth, and integrity, which are essential for thriving in volatile and unpredictable markets. This discipline transforms ambitions into achievements and ensures meaningful progress.

While the components of Niyama may appear overlapping, each principle remains distinct yet interconnected. Together, they form a cohesive framework that supports holistic leadership and personal development, creating a solid foundation for navigating the complexities of modern business. Let us explore each Niyama through the lens of contemporary business practices and leadership principles.

Saucha (Self-Purification)

Saucha (*saw-chuh*) literally translates to performing ablutions. However, under Yogic philosophy, it extends far beyond this and includes the cleansing of both tangible and intangible aspects of our lives—the body, personal spaces, words, and thoughts. As Virginia Smith explores in her very interesting book *Clean: A History of Personal Hygiene and Purity*, maintaining personal and environmental cleanliness has long been recognized as fundamental to societal progress and individual well-being.

Tangible Purification: Saucha begins with maintaining cleanliness of the body and surroundings. Simple practices, such as bathing before starting work—whether at home or in an office—and wearing clean clothes, demonstrate respect and professionalism while promoting physical and mental well-being. Bathing enhances blood circulation, relaxes muscles, and refreshes the mind, instilling a sense of readiness and energy to approach the day effectively. Even in remote work settings, starting the day with a shower and fresh attire can boost energy and enhance productivity. Similarly, keeping personal workspaces tidy fosters mental clarity and focus. A clean and organized environment reflects inner discipline and contributes to a sense of calm and purpose, creating spaces that inspire both focus and productivity.

Intangible Purification: Negative thoughts, especially grudges, keep us anchored in the past, while anxieties pull us into the future, clouding judgment and hindering decision-making. When we practice Saucha, we focus on actively cleansing the mind of distractions, allowing us to stay present and achieve the mental clarity necessary for sound decisions and effective leadership.

A crucial aspect of intangible purification is refining one's language. Words originate from thoughts, and the words we use shape how we are perceived while directly influencing the effectiveness of our communication. Confucius wisely noted that understanding the power of words is essential to gaining deeper knowledge, a sentiment reflected in the Sanskrit concept of *Shabda Brahma*. Words possess the power to build or destroy, with the ability to undo years of effort in mere seconds.

Using inappropriate language—such as profanities or overly casual expressions in formal settings—can erode credibility and professionalism. However, purity of language is not about displaying an extensive vocabulary but about understanding the weight of words and wielding them thoughtfully and skillfully.

In negotiations or diplomacy, the choice of words becomes even more critical. Words can diffuse tension, build bridges, or escalate conflicts. As the Bee Gees beautifully captured in one of my favorite songs, *Words*, "*Talk in everlasting words.*" These lyrics have always resonated deeply with me, reminding me of the immense power of language to shape connections and outcomes. For example, one US President faced criticism for using street language that resonated with a few but alienated many more, especially in professional or diplomatic contexts. In contrast, leaders like Prime Minister Narendra Modi demonstrate the art of refined and impactful communication, inspiring trust and commanding respect on a global stage. It is a powerful reminder of how thoughtful words can foster collaboration and understanding.

By embracing Saucha, we lay the foundation of respect, professionalism, and trust. This principle nurtures meaningful relationships, fosters productive interactions, and creates a harmonious balance between the tangible and intangible aspects of life.

Santosha (Contentment)

Santosha (*sun-toe-sha*) is the practice of contentment—finding satisfaction in what we have while nurturing healthy ambition. It does not imply abandoning aspirations or settling for less but instead encourages releasing the relentless chase for more and discovering peace in the present moment. In business, this Niyama guides us to balance ambition with gratitude, recognizing that success is not only about constant striving but also about appreciating our current achievements. It is about pursuing goals with intention while avoiding the pitfalls of burnout or perpetual dissatisfaction. By embodying Santosha, we learn when to pause, reflect, and accept what lies beyond our control, creating a healthier, more sustainable, and more fulfilling work environment.

Employee burnout, a growing challenge in many organizations, underscores the importance of cultivating Santosha. Research published in the *Journal of Public Administration Research and Theory* highlights that burnout contributes to increased absenteeism, reduced productivity, and higher employee turnover. A systematic review in *PLOS ONE*, a peer-reviewed open-access scientific journal, further emphasizes the long-term health consequences of burnout and its negative impact on organizational performance. By embracing the principles of Santosha, we can foster work cultures that prioritize mental and emotional well-being, mitigating burnout while enhancing employee retention and productivity.

A strong example of Santosha in business is Basecamp, led by Jason Fried and David Heinemeier Hansson. The company is renowned for its intentional approach to fostering a calm work culture and avoiding the relentless pursuit of hyper-growth. Fried and Hansson emphasize the value of sustainable, steady growth and contentment with the current state of the business, prioritizing excellence over speed. Their book *It Does Not Have to Be Crazy at Work* advocates for a balanced and thoughtful approach to growth that places employee well-being and long-term success at the forefront.

The ideas presented in *Small Giants: Companies That Choose to Be Great Instead of Big* by Bo Burlingham align deeply with the principle of Santosha. The book highlights companies that have deliberately chosen excellence and a fulfilling work environment over rapid expansion. These businesses prioritize quality, employee satisfaction, and community impact, embodying the essence of Santosha by finding contentment in their current state while nurturing meaningful growth. Burlingham's insights remind us that true success is not always measured by size, but by the depth of purpose and satisfaction within an organization.

By fostering this kind of contentment, companies like Basecamp and the businesses featured in *Small Giants* have cultivated loyal customer bases and positive work cultures. This approach demonstrates that steady, mindful growth is just as valuable as rapid expansion, reflecting the principle of Santosha, which encourages us to release excessive ambition and focus on sustainable, high-quality outcomes.

Tapas (Self-Discipline)

Tapas (*tuh-pus*), meaning "heat" or "ardor," embodies the principles of self-discipline, perseverance, and steadfast commitment to personal and professional growth. In the business realm, Tapas is evident in the unwavering dedication to challenging tasks, the resolve to make difficult decisions, and the resilience to pursue long-term objectives despite obstacles.

A compelling example of Tapas is found in Angela Duckworth's book, *Grit: The Power of Passion and Perseverance*. Duckworth delves into how individuals who demonstrate a blend of passion and sustained persistence—qualities that lie at the heart of Tapas—achieve extraordinary success. She argues that talent alone is not enough; what truly sets high achievers apart is their ability to apply consistent effort and determination over time. This perspective resonates deeply with the essence of Tapas, underscoring the transformative power of enduring commitment and self-discipline in turning aspirations into reality.

Embracing Tapas means developing resilience and maintaining focus in the face of uncertainty, setbacks, and challenges. It involves a daily commitment to progress, the courage to make difficult decisions that prioritize long-term gains over short-term rewards, and the discipline to stay the course even when immediate results are not visible. Tapas encourages us to persevere through adversity with steadfast resolve, creating opportunities for personal growth, innovation, and lasting success. Moreover, by embodying Tapas, we can inspire those around us to adopt a similar mindset, fostering work environments where challenges are viewed as stepping stones to growth and collective achievements.

Swadhyaya (Self-Study and Self-Reflection)

Swadhyaya (*swa-dhy-a-ya*), or self-study and self-reflection, is essential for personal and professional growth. In the workplace, it translates to developing self-awareness—a crucial trait for effective leadership. Engaging in regular self-assessment allows us to evaluate our motivations, strengths, and areas for improvement, ensuring continuous evolution and better decision-making.

Practices such as journaling, personal reflection, and seeking feedback through methods like 360-degree reviews help uncover blind spots and biases, fostering personal and professional growth. One highly effective method for practicing Swadhyaya is holding a meeting with oneself. Similar to a formal business meeting, this self-meeting should have a clear, structured agenda and include time for honest reflection and introspection. It begins by reviewing the minutes from the previous self-meeting, noting progress on earlier goals or commitments. This habit of self-review helps maintain accountability, track growth over time, and make meaningful adjustments.

The Johari Window, developed by psychologists Joseph Luft and Harrington Ingham, provides a structured framework for practicing Swadhyaya. It is divided into four quadrants that represent different aspects of self-awareness and interpersonal dynamics:

1. **Open Area**: Known to both self and others. This is the area of transparency, collaboration, and trust. Expanding this area strengthens relationships and communication.

2. **Blind Area**: Known to others but not to self. This is often referred to as the "area for potential improvement," as feedback from others can illuminate blind spots and help individuals grow.

3. **Hidden Area**: Known to self but not to others. This is sometimes called the "hypocrite zone" when individuals withhold key aspects of themselves, which can hinder authenticity and trust. Reducing this area involves sharing more openly with others.

4. **Unknown Area**: Unknown to both self and others. This is the area of untapped potential, unexplored possibilities, or unconscious traits. Personal growth and exploration gradually reveal parts of this quadrant.

Regular feedback and introspection help shrink the Blind and Hidden Areas while expanding the Open Area. This fosters self-awareness, improves relationships, and enhances leadership effectiveness.

Below is the matrix representation with these expanded labels:

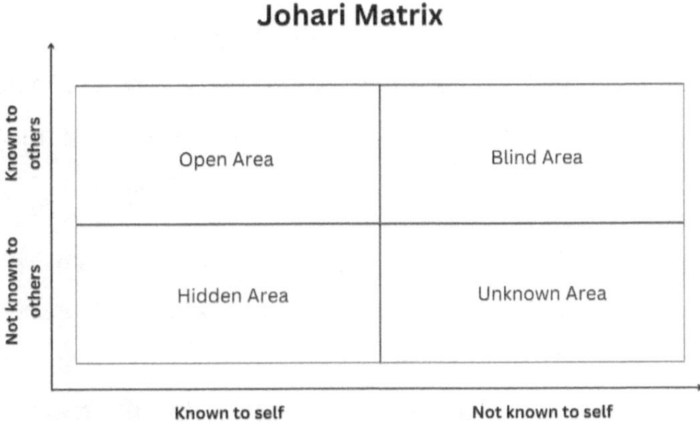

The importance of ongoing self-reflection in leadership is emphasized by Peter Drucker, who stated, "Follow effective action with quiet reflection. From the quiet reflection will come even more effective action." This illustrates how Swadhyaya enhances decision-making and future performance.

Executive education programs are another example of Swadhyaya in action, offering structured opportunities for self-reflection and skill development. These programs help professionals contextualize theoretical knowledge within real-world scenarios, leading to practical insights that can be immediately applied. In his seminal book, *The 7 Habits of Highly Effective People*, Stephen Covey refers to this practice as Sharpening the Saw—the habit of continuous self-improvement that keeps one relevant.

The concept is further reflected in mandatory continuing professional education required for maintaining certain professional qualifications. This ensures that individuals stay updated with evolving knowledge and are equipped to address industry challenges effectively. By emphasizing smart work over aimless hard work, professionals can remain adaptable, relevant, and impactful in their fields.

A powerful example of Swadhyaya is Warren Buffett, who credits much of his success to a disciplined practice of reading and self-reflection. Buffett dedicates a significant portion of his day to reading, considering it essential for expanding knowledge and sharpening perspective. Similarly, Bill Gates incorporates extensive reading into his routine, recognizing it as a cornerstone of his growth and success. Younger leaders like Alexandra Cavoulacos, co-founder of The Muse, and Ankur Warikoo, founder of Nearbuy and author of the engaging *Do Epic Shit*, also prioritize regular reading and introspection, showcasing the enduring relevance of Swadhyaya in leadership and personal growth.

Ishvara Pranidhana (Surrender to a Superior Power)

Ishvara Pranidhana (*Ish-va-ra Pra-ni-dha-na*) refers to the practice of surrendering to a higher power or force beyond oneself. It is important to note that Ishvara is not confined to any specific religion. In Sanskrit, 'Ish' means 'capable of,' and 'vara' signifies 'choice' or 'wish,' collectively representing the capability to choose and the power of will. Ishvara, ultimately, is our own chosen power, embodying the source we personally trust and revere. This Niyama encourages us to trust the process and recognize that not everything is within our control, whether it involves surrendering to an inner voice, an external guide, or a higher concept of divinity.

In today's context, this idea resonates even with postmodern thinkers who question the nature of reality itself. Some propose that our existence could be part of a highly advanced simulation or an AI-driven reality—another interpretation of a force greater than ourselves. While such theories may seem speculative, they embody the essence of Ishvara Pranidhana by inviting us to embrace the unknown and trust in a broader structure or force beyond our comprehension.

In my own life, I have found profound comfort in surrendering to Krishna as my chosen Ishvara. Whether or not Krishna exists in a tangible sense, I have embraced Him as my Supreme Friend and entrusted my anxieties to Him. It is a simple yet transformative philosophy: "Do what you do best and outsource the rest!" This practice of letting go of control—while retaining ambition—instills in me the confidence to take the next step, secure in the belief that I have placed my trust in something far greater than myself.

In business, Ishvara Pranidhana is about letting go of the need to control everything. Leaders who embrace this

Niyama understand that micromanaging every aspect of an organization is neither practical nor effective. Instead, they focus on delegating responsibilities, trusting their teams' capabilities, and having faith in the larger process. This practice of surrender does not signify passivity or complacency but reflects the wisdom to recognize when to step back and allow creativity and collaboration to thrive.

A profound example of spiritual surrender in leadership comes from Steve Jobs. Deeply influenced by Zen Buddhism, his visit to India, and the teachings of Neem Karoli Baba, Jobs experienced a shift in perspective that shaped his life and leadership. Although he arrived at Neem Karoli Baba's Kainchi Dham ashram after the Baba's passing, the journey left an indelible mark on his thinking. Jobs often spoke about trusting the process and embracing uncertainty. His well-known insight, "You can't connect the dots looking forward; you can only connect them looking backward. So you have to trust that the dots will somehow connect in your future," reflects the essence of Ishvara Pranidhana. This philosophy guided bold decisions at Apple, such as the launch of the revolutionary iPhone. Jobs's ability to trust intuition and creativity over rigid control became a defining trait of his visionary leadership.

Notably, Jobs's spiritual journey left a ripple effect; he later suggested that Mark Zuckerberg visit Neem Karoli Baba's ashram for inspiration. Zuckerberg, in a conversation with Indian Prime Minister Narendra Modi, acknowledged the transformative impact of his visit to the ashram. This connection illustrates how spiritual surrender can influence not only personal leadership but also inspire others to seek clarity and purpose.

In essence, Ishvara Pranidhana is about trusting the larger process and understanding when to let go of control. Whether it is faith in a divine force, as in my case with Krishna, or a philosophical approach like Steve Jobs's trust in the unknown, surrender empowers leaders to take risks, innovate, and inspire those around them. By releasing the need for micromanagement, we create an environment that fosters collaboration, creativity, and sustainable success.

This powerful concept is further explored by Dr. Judith Orloff in *The Ecstasy of Surrender*, where she examines the transformative power of surrendering to a higher power. Dr. Orloff explains that surrender is not about giving up or being passive but about letting go of the need to control everything. It is about trusting in the flow of life and allowing ourselves to be guided by a higher energy, whether it be the universe, divine wisdom, or our inner guidance. She highlights how surrender can lead to greater emotional freedom, reduce stress, and foster deeper connections with others. By relinquishing control, we create space for personal transformation, healing, and growth. Dr. Orloff also offers practical exercises to help individuals move beyond fear and limiting beliefs, encouraging them to trust in life's natural flow. Surrendering to a higher power unlocks immense potential, enabling us to experience peace, joy, and a deeper sense of fulfillment in both our personal and professional lives.

Practical Approach to Yama and Niyama

Step 1: Begin with the WHY

- Reflect on your purpose: Why are you doing what you are doing?
- Write a personal mission statement and evaluate whether it aligns with the mission of the business you lead or contribute to.

Step 2: Commit to the Practice

- For 28 days (the ancient Yogic practice, now scientifically recognized as a 28-day timeframe required for forming habits), dedicate just 10 minutes daily journaling about the five Yamas and five Niyamas.
- Focus on what you accomplished each day. Ignore what you did not.

Yama (The Principles)

1. Ahimsa (Non-violence): Note one instance where you practiced non-violence, including verbal non-violence

or choosing vegetarian food, even when provoked or tempted.

2. Satya (Truthfulness): Record a truth you upheld, despite immediate incentives to the contrary.

3. Asteya (Non-stealing): Reflect on a moment where you credited someone for even the smallest contribution. Rhetorical thank-yous do not count.

4. Aparigraha (Non-possessiveness): Identify one piece of clutter—physical, emotional, or mental—that you let go of.

5. Brahmacharya (Moderation): Highlight one urge you controlled, enabling you to focus on your values.

Niyama (The Discipline)

1. Shaucha (Self-Purification): Record one way you kept your body, surroundings, or thoughts clean today. Routine ablutions do not count.

2. Santosha (Contentment): Note one moment of gratitude or contentment you experienced.

3. Tapas (Self-Discipline): Note one disciplined action or habit you maintained. Discipline is choosing between what you want now and what you want most.

4. Swadhyaya (Self-study): Reflect on one lesson learned from introspection or your work.

5. Ishwara Pranidhana (Surrender): Record one worry or burden you released by trusting the process or a higher power.

Step 3: Reflect and Grow

- After 28 days, review your journal entries and summarize your experience.
- Identify areas for improvement and recognize actions that brought positive change.
- Reward yourself if you are satisfied with your progress—celebrating small wins matters.
- Share your results with someone you trust, creating a safe space to be vulnerable. Social media is not that place.
- Develop a personalized self-assessment mechanism to sustain and deepen your practice.

Asana
(The Posture)

Asana, the physical posture in Yoga, is perhaps its most visible and popular aspect, primarily because of the immediate benefits it confers on the body. However, it is just a preparatory stage for the ultimate goal of Yoga. According to the Yoga Sutras of Patanjali, *"Sthira Sukham Asanam"* emphasizes that Asana is about achieving a balance between stability and ease. It serves as a crucial foundation, preparing the body and mind for deeper spiritual and mental development.

The human body is not merely a vehicle for enjoying material comforts; it is a vessel for human consciousness, often referred to as the soul—an antenna designed to receive signals from universal transmitters. For this vehicle to move smoothly and the antenna to function optimally, it must be prepared and attuned to the right frequency—a task addressed by the physical practices of yoga, including Asana. When practiced consistently, Asanas open energy channels, harmonize internal systems, and enhance the body's resilience and flexibility, ensuring it is receptive to the higher frequencies of energy that the Universe has to offer.

In this context, Asana transcends being a mere physical exercise. It becomes a method of harmonizing the body, mind, and consciousness, enabling one to connect with the universal flow of energy and intuition. For this reception to work, the body must be balanced with strength and flexibility, free of energy blockages.

Asana mirrors the interplay of dualities that leaders and organizations must navigate. Just as a yoga posture demands stability with ease, so too must businesses balance competing yet complementary forces to thrive. Stability with flexibility, endurance with focus, consistency with adaptability, and vision with execution are examples of such dualities. Mastering these dualities ensures that we remain grounded yet agile, resilient yet innovative.

A Practical Approach to Asana

This book is not primarily a manual on physical practices, so I will not dwell extensively on this aspect of yoga. However, no discussion of yoga is complete without acknowledging its physical dimension. The following section offers a simple framework of 25 Asanas, designed to fit into even the busiest of schedules. By dedicating just 40 minutes out of the 1,440 minutes in a day, we can unlock the immense potential of our body to function as an efficient vehicle and an effective antenna, ready to connect with the higher energies transmitted through the Universe.

The selected Asanas are simple and accessible for people of all fitness levels, organized into five categories, each focusing on a specific aspect of well-being. There is no need to visit a yoga studio or have a dedicated instructor or Guru to begin practicing these straightforward poses. Choose two Asanas from each series, rotate them periodically, and practice them consistently, nearly every day. Practicing only once a week, as yoga studios would have you do, is like eating just once a week—it simply will not provide the lasting benefits you need. These poses require minimal equipment; even a fresh towel can replace a yoga mat when traveling. At home, covering your yoga mat with a clean towel ensures hygiene and adds a sense of renewal to your practice. Ideally, practice on an empty stomach, fasting for at least four hours beforehand, and aim for a time between 4:00 AM and 6:00 PM.

Until the practice becomes a regular and cherished part of your routine—addictive in the positive sense of the word—try to practice with a friend, even over a video call. This creates a sense of accountability and combats the natural human tendency to procrastinate. Believe me, you are not alone in putting things off, but having a partner brings both commitment and encouragement to stay consistent. This small step of building mutual motivation can transform your practice into a sustainable and rewarding habit.

Structure of the Practice:

1. **Warm-Up (5 minutes):** Begin with light exercises such as Surya Namaskar (Sun Salutation), breathing exercises, or other free-hand warm-ups to prepare the body. (Look at the figures provided in Appendix 4 for the twelve postures needed to do Surya Namaskar).

2. **Asana Practice (25 minutes):** Select two postures from each of the five series outlined in Appendix 5. Each pose blends physical benefits with mindfulness, the key elements for transitioning from compulsiveness to consciousness. This combination makes them ideal for building a strong foundation for both yoga practice and personal and business stability. Illustrations for these poses are included in the same appendix.

3. **Pranayama (10 minutes):** This will be covered in detail in the next chapter, exploring the fourth limb of Ashtanga Yoga.

Pranayama
(The Control over Life Force)

Pranayama (*pra-na-ya-ma*), the fourth and the most important limb of Ashtanga Yoga, is far more than simply "breath control" or "breathing exercises." It is a deeply integrated practice that regulates the flow of vital energy (Prana) within the body. The term Pranayama is derived from two Sanskrit words—Prana, meaning life force or vital energy, and Ayama, meaning control. This life force connects every cell in the body, giving us the sense of being a unified whole. When this energy is interrupted or depleted, the body ceases to function effectively. Therefore, Pranayama is the ability to control Prana, with the breath being the most immediate and accessible form of this energy.

Breath and Mind Connection

By gaining control over our breath, we gain control over our Prana, which in turn allows us to extend that control to the mind, emotions, and ultimately, our actions. The breath serves as the bridge between the body and the mind, and when we master it, we achieve a powerful means of directing our energy. This is particularly vital in the workplace, where focus, emotional regulation, and mental clarity are essential for successful decision-making and leadership.

The Mind vs. The Brain

Modern science often uses the terms "mind" and "brain" interchangeably, but in yogic philosophy, they are distinct. The brain is the physical organ that can be studied, measured, and mapped using tools like EEG, while the mind is a formless, energetic field shaped by thinking, feeling, and choosing. The mind has the ability to create and direct energy by focusing on specific tasks, emotions, or ideas. This is why attention is such a powerful tool—energy flows where attention goes. In yoga, control over the mind is paramount because a distracted, uncontrolled mind dissipates energy, making it impossible to achieve focused goals, whether in life or business.

Energy and High Performance

The practice of Pranayama translates into controlling one's mental energy and directing it effectively. By mastering Pranayama, we can develop a calm and focused mind, which enhances our ability to manage stress, make strategic decisions, and lead with clarity.

"Energy, not time, is the fundamental currency of high performance," says Jim Loehr in *The Power of Full Engagement*. This principle aligns seamlessly with the essence of Pranayama. Loehr identifies four dimensions of energy—physical, emotional, mental, and spiritual—and emphasizes that achieving full engagement requires optimizing all four. This involves not only building energetic capacity but also ensuring adequate recovery. At work, leaders often prioritize time management, but true effectiveness stems from mastering energy management—a core tenet of Pranayama, which focuses on channeling and regulating energy through breath and mindful awareness.

Similarly, in *Energy Leadership: The 7 Level Framework for Mastery in Life and Business*, Bruce D. Schneider explores how understanding and harnessing personal energy can transform leadership effectiveness. He introduces a framework that closely aligns with the principles of Pranayama, advocating for conscious energy management to achieve peak performance. Schneider asserts that Energy Leadership can be applied to various aspects of life, including work, relationships, and personal growth.

The Life Force of an Organization

For us to live, breathing is essential, but can it be the purpose of living? Similarly, for businesses to thrive, they must generate profit—even not-for-profit organizations must ensure an excess of income over expenses. Yet, profit cannot be the Prana or the life force of a business. Breathing sustains life as a vital force, and controlling this force, as Pranayama does, unlocks greater potential. In the same way, businesses must identify the life force that propels their success and manage it with intention. Many businesses become so preoccupied with operational efficiency and profitability that they lose sight of their true life force and purpose.

While customers might seem to be the life force of any business, no one, including monopolies, can directly control their customers. What they can control is the process of attracting and retaining them. The true life force of a business lies in these processes, which must align with its purpose and values. Consider EasyJet, a pioneer in transforming the airline reservation experience. By developing an exceptionally simple and user-friendly interface, the airline made travel planning literally 'easy' for its customers. This innovative process became their life force, enabling them to deliver consistent value while remaining true to their purpose of making air travel accessible and hassle-free.

Take Spotify, whose life force lies in ensuring musicians receive the dues they deserve while offering users a piracy-free listening experience. At one stroke, Spotify achieved what no government legislation or harsh penalties ever could: eliminate music piracy. While governments focused on strengthening laws and enforcing stricter punishments to combat piracy, Spotify's innovative technology and purpose-driven model addressed the root cause. By providing affordable, seamless access to music, Spotify orchestrated its business process with its life force, creating a win-win for artists and listeners alike.

Identifying Our Business' Prana

Like EasyJet or Spotify, businesses must identify their Prana—their life force—and ensure they have control over it. Prana often lies beneath what is most apparent: an IKEA's flat-packed furniture and efficient self-service model that improves indoor living standards wherever they go; a Canva's platform that transforms a non-designer into a designer; a Shopify's user interface (UI) that simplifies e-commerce, giving great user experience (UX) to entrepreneurs and their customers alike; or a Virtuo's keyless, personless car rental experience that redefines customer experience (CX) for a business as analog as renting cars. Zoom's Prana is its grandma-friendly interface that has turned video conferencing into a household verb, while countless other businesses derive their life force from equally understated yet critical aspects.

The deeper we study, the more evident it becomes that Customer Experience (CX) is the true Prana for a business— not the customers themselves, not the products they offer, nor their competitive positioning. CX is the life force that drives customer loyalty, brand perception, and long-term success. Just like the product we sell must be designed, the CX too must be designed. Unlike products or services, CX is a feeling. So how can feelings be designed? Feelings are designed by orchestrating memorable moments that resonate emotionally. As Maya Angelou said, "People will forget what you said, people will forget what you did, but people will never forget how you made them feel."

Designing the Prana - Customer Experience (CX)

Designing CX involves crafting interactions that leave a lasting emotional impact. While products or services are tangible, CX is an intangible feeling created through empathy, thoughtful planning, and purposeful actions. Designing the Prana or the CX of a business requires the following steps:

Customer Journey Mapping: Just as Pranayama requires mindful control and direction of the breath, designing an exceptional Customer Experience (CX) requires a purposeful approach to customer interactions. Mapping the customer journey and identifying key touchpoints allows businesses to create moments that evoke trust and satisfaction. Interestingly, customer experience is often inversely proportional to the number of touchpoints—the fewer the touchpoints, the more seamless the experience. For example, at Apple Stores, the same person who gives the product demo also serves as the cashier once you decide to make a purchase. This creates a smoother, more efficient experience, much like a smooth, controlled breath in Pranayama.

Personalization: Pranayama is about tuning into your own energy and directing it with intention. Similarly, personalization in CX involves understanding individual customer needs and preferences to create a tailored experience. Companies like Netflix, Spotify, and Amazon excel in using customer data to suggest personalized content, products, or services. This data-driven approach makes customers feel genuinely valued, much like Pranayama's focus on using energy consciously to create specific outcomes. When customers feel understood and catered to, they develop a deeper connection with the brand.

Sensory Design: Just as Pranayama engages the breath to create a focused, balanced mind and body, businesses can use sensory design to engage customers on an emotional level. Companies like Tesla and Disney excel at sensory design by incorporating visuals, sounds, and other sensory elements that enhance emotional engagement. Tesla's minimalist interiors and seamless technology evoke calm and innovation, while Disney's immersive themed environments, enchanting scents, and captivating sounds create unforgettable emotional connections. This sensory engagement mirrors the transformative power of Pranayama, where energy is channeled to evoke a positive and lasting impact.

Feedback and Iteration: Pranayama requires consistent practice and reflection to deepen the connection with one's breath, just as CX design requires continuous feedback and iteration. Using tools like Net Promoter Score (NPS) allows businesses to gather customer insights and fine-tune their customer interactions. This iterative process ensures that CX evolves to meet customer needs, much like the ongoing practice of Pranayama strengthens the mind-body connection over time.

The four steps above share a common goal—curating emotionally resonant moments that foster loyalty and trust. By treating CX as a deliberate and purposeful creation, rather than a mere incidental outcome, we can build businesses that can forge enduring connections and 'breathe' Prana into themselves.

The Interconnection of EX, SX, and CoX in CX

CX is intrinsically tied to Employee Experience (EX), Supplier Experience (SX), and Community Experience (CoX). Employee Experience determines the energy, engagement, and commitment employees bring to delivering exceptional CX. This, in turn, depends on their level of consciousness—an awakened inner compass that empowers employees to act with purpose and intuition, rather than through mere compulsion. Compulsiveness, driven by external factors like regulations, rewards, or penalties, is fundamentally different from consciousness, which arises from listening to inner guidance. Yoga, particularly Pranayama, offers an ancient methodology to raise levels of consciousness, helping individuals overcome compulsiveness. And since consciousness, by its very nature, is non-material, one must ask: can something immaterial be driven by material incentives? The answer lies in cultivating consciousness within employees, enabling them to contribute meaningfully to CX.

As the old adage goes, "Things well bought are already half sold." Supplier Experience (SX) is another vital aspect of CX. Suppliers form the lifeblood of operational success, contributing directly to a business's ability to deliver quality products and services. A supplier who is valued, respected, and well-supported is far more likely to bring innovation, reliability, and efficiency to the table. Conversely, treating suppliers as easily replaceable cogs in a machine stifles their potential for collaboration and creativity, which ultimately impacts CX. Businesses that nurture SX build stronger, more reliable supply chains that benefit both operations and customer satisfaction.

Community Experience (CoX) is equally crucial, though often overlooked. Communities are not direct customers or suppliers, but they are profoundly affected by the actions and inactions of a business. A business that pollutes its environment, disrupts local life, or drains resources alienates its community, negatively impacting how employees, customers, and suppliers perceive it. Conversely, businesses that invest in supporting local initiatives, promoting social development, and contributing to the well-being of their communities gain not only social capital but also trust and respect that extends far beyond their geographical reach. Communities are silent stakeholders in every business, and their experience forms the foundation of long-term sustainability and goodwill.

While EX, SX, and CoX may not individually be the Prana of a business, they are inextricably intertwined with CX, which is the ultimate life force. Businesses that fail to recognize and nurture these interconnected experiences risk compromising their Prana, weakening their ability to create lasting impact and value. On the other hand, those that balance and elevate all these experiences cultivate a harmonious ecosystem where purpose, innovation, and success flourish together.

Practical Approach to Pranayama

Just like Asanas, Pranayama is one of the most commonly known and practiced aspects of Yoga. However, it is also just a stepping stone toward the ultimate goal of Yoga. Pranayama is best practiced after completing your Asanas, as it helps calm the mind and energize the body. The minimum duration for this practice is just 10 minutes, though extending it will offer even greater benefits. Below are four simple yet powerful Pranayamas that can be practiced daily.

Sheetali Pranayama (Cooling Breath)

Duration: 1 Minute

Process:

1. Sit comfortably with your back straight and shoulders relaxed.
2. Roll your tongue into a tube shape and extend it slightly out of your mouth.
3. Inhale deeply through the tube-like tongue for about 10 seconds, allowing the cool air to enter your body.
4. Close your mouth and exhale slowly through your nose for about 5 seconds.
5. Repeat this cycle four times.

Benefits:

- Alleviates inflammation, providing relief similar to the cooling effects of a cold water dip.
- Reduces body heat, making it effective during hot weather or after physical exertion.
- Calms the mind, alleviating stress and promoting a sense of tranquility.
- Helps with anger management by cooling emotional agitation.

A study published in the *Journal of Complementary and Integrative Medicine* (De Gruyter, Germany, 2021) highlights significant benefits of Sheetali Pranayam. This breathing technique effectively reduces body temperature, alleviates inflammation, and calms the nervous system. It is particularly beneficial for managing stress-related disorders and improving emotional regulation. The findings also indicate enhanced parasympathetic activity, promoting relaxation and better sleep quality. Additionally, Sheetali Pranayam supports digestive health by reducing acidity and aiding in detoxification. These results affirm its role as a holistic practice for mental, physical, and emotional well-being, key attributes for successful leadership.

Anulom Vilom Pranayama (Alternate Nostril Breathing)

Duration: At least 7 Minutes

Process:

1. Sit comfortably in a meditative posture with your back straight and shoulders relaxed.
2. Close your right nostril gently with your thumb and inhale deeply through your left nostril for about 4 seconds.
3. Close your left nostril with your ring finger, release your thumb from the right nostril, and exhale slowly through the right nostril for about 4 seconds.
4. Inhale through the right nostril for 4 seconds, then close it with your thumb and exhale through the left nostril for 4 seconds.

5. Repeat this alternate nostril breathing pattern for a minimum of seven minutes, ensuring your inhalation is smooth and your exhalation slower and controlled.

Benefits:

- Balances Ida (calming energy) and Pingala (active energy), harmonizing the body's energies for mental clarity and emotional balance.
- Enhances focus and concentration, making it ideal for leaders and decision-makers.
- Calms the nervous system, alleviating stress and reducing symptoms of anxiety.
- Improves lung function, boosting oxygen exchange and respiratory efficiency.
- Promotes mindfulness and steadies the mind, creating a foundation for meditation and inner peace.

This is regarded as the most significant of all Pranayamas due to its profound impact on both physical and mental well-being. Anulom Vilom acts as a bridge between the physical and spiritual, grounding the practitioner while preparing the mind for deeper states of awareness. It has been recognized for its ability to balance the autonomic nervous system, reduce stress, and enhance overall well-being. A 2018 study published in *Frontiers in Human Neuroscience* by researchers from the University of Pisa, Italy, highlighted the benefits of alternate nostril breathing. The research demonstrated improvements in autonomic function, emotional stability, and stress reduction. This pranayama harmonizes Ida (calming energy) and Pingala (active energy), promoting mental clarity and emotional balance. Practicing this technique regularly not only strengthens lung function but also calms the nervous system, offering a gateway to greater focus and resilience in both personal and professional life.

Bhramari Pranayama (Humming Bee Breath)

Duration: 1 Minute

Process:

1. Sit in a comfortable position with your back straight.
2. Close your eyes and gently place your index fingers on your ears to block external noise.
3. Inhale deeply through your nose for about 5 seconds.
4. Exhale slowly through your nose for about 10 seconds while producing a gentle humming sound, like a bee.
5. Repeat this process four times.

Benefits:

- Relieves stress, tension, and mental agitation.
- Enhances focus and concentration by calming the mind.
- Induces a meditative state, making it easier to transition into deeper meditation practices.
- Promotes emotional stability by reducing symptoms of anxiety and restlessness.

Bhramari Pranayama has been shown to significantly increase the production of nitric oxide (NO) in the body.

A study published in the *Indian Journal of Science and Technology* (2023) reported that humming during exhalation, a key component of Bhramari Pranayama, can increase nasal NO levels by up to 15 times compared to quiet exhalation. This surge in NO production enhances vasodilation, improving blood flow and oxygen delivery throughout the body. Additionally, elevated NO levels play a crucial role in immune defense by exhibiting antimicrobial properties, thereby supporting respiratory health. Regular practice of Bhramari Pranayama not only promotes relaxation and stress reduction but also leverages the therapeutic benefits of increased nitric oxide production, contributing to overall cardiovascular and respiratory well-being.

Udgeet Pranayama (Chanting Breath)

Duration: 1 Minute

Process:

1. Sit in a comfortable meditative posture with your spine erect.
2. Inhale deeply through your nose for about 4 seconds.
3. As you exhale slowly, chant the mantra "Om" in a long, steady tone.
   - Let the "O" sound resonate for about 75% of the exhalation and the "M" sound for the remaining 25%.
   - The exhalation should last approximately 8 seconds.
4. Repeat this process four times.

Benefits:

- Promotes calmness and emotional equilibrium by soothing the nervous system.
- Balances the mind with positive vibrations, enhancing inner peace and spiritual awareness.
- Improves mental clarity, making it an ideal practice for reducing distractions.
- Strengthens the lungs and enhances the quality of breathing.

A study conducted by researchers at the National Institute of Mental Health and Neurosciences (NIMHANS) in Bangalore, India, and published in the *International Journal of Yoga* (2011), highlights the profound impact of Udgeet Pranayama. Using functional MRI scans, the research revealed that chanting "Om" deactivates the limbic system, particularly the amygdala, a brain region associated with stress and emotional processing. This deactivation triggers a relaxation response in the body, reducing physiological markers of stress, enhancing emotional stability, and promoting an overall sense of calm. The findings underscore Udgeet Pranayama's ability to bring clarity and tranquility to the mind, making it an invaluable tool for individuals seeking to channelize their energy and find balance amidst life's demands.

Practicing the four Pranayamas—Sheetali, Anulom Vilom, Bhramari, and Udgeet—in sequence offers a comprehensive approach to nurturing physical, mental, and emotional well-being. Devoting just 10 minutes a day to these techniques promotes balance, sharpens focus, and revitalizes both body and mind, laying the groundwork for harmony and vitality.

Pratyahara
(The Art of Letting Go)

"Some of us think holding on makes us strong; but sometimes it is letting go," said Hermann Hesse, the Nobel Laureate in Literature, whose works profoundly influenced modern thought. This encapsulates the essence of Pratyahara (*prut-ya-hara*), the fifth limb of Ashtanga Yoga, which emphasizes "withdrawal from intake" by turning the senses inward to reduce distractions and cultivate mindfulness. In a modern context, it involves letting go of unproductive thoughts, technology, processes, and people, helping us to focus on what truly matters.

Withdrawing from Distractions

The first and easiest step in Pratyahara is the withdrawal from thoughts that cause unnecessary distraction, especially negative and self-limiting ones. The human mind, like an untamed monkey, often becomes entangled in a web of unproductive, repetitive, and pessimistic thoughts. These patterns drain energy, stifle creativity, and create barriers to both personal and professional progress. Practicing Pratyahara encourages a mindful approach—acknowledging the presence of such thoughts without judgment and consciously choosing to release them. This deliberate act of letting go fosters mental clarity and emotional balance, paving the way for positivity, creativity, and purposeful action to flourish.

Technology: A Simple Area for Pratyahara

Technology comes next, and it is one of the easiest areas to practice Pratyahara. Outdated or irrelevant technology not only becomes a distraction but also a major barrier to progress. Imagine using a typewriter instead of a computer, or a clothes beater instead of a washing machine; or navigating with a paper map instead of a GPS! Whether at home or at the workplace, it is crucial to withdraw from such obsolete tools and systems. By identifying and eliminating these inefficiencies, businesses and individuals can energize innovation, streamline efforts, and maintain productivity in an ever-changing environment.

The Challenge of Outdated Habits and Processes

The Pratyahara of processes for businesses and habits for individuals presents a slightly greater challenge. As creatures of habit, we often hold on to routines that, over time, lose their relevance and hinder personal growth. Practicing Pratyahara means consciously stepping back, releasing outdated habits, and embracing new, purposeful ones. James Clear's *Atomic Habits* offers a practical framework for this transformation, demonstrating how small, consistent changes can yield significant results. Breaking bad habits, on the other hand, requires reversing the principles of behavior change. By adopting new, productive habits, we naturally phase out the old, unproductive ones.

The Kafkaesque Struggle: All of us have faced one—a Kafkaesque nightmare born of entrenched bureaucracy and rigid processes, where simple tasks become exercises in frustration. Over time, many organizations, not only inadvertently but sometimes through deliberate neglect, create such environments, alienating their lifeblood—the customers. This requires businesses to step back, reassess, and eliminate inefficiencies that no longer serve their values or purpose. Consider the tragic case of Brian Thompson, CEO of UnitedHealthcare, a company insuring 50 million Americans, whose shocking murder underscores the depths of frustration and despair bred by bureaucratic absurdity.

A Kafkaesque battle, as Franz Kafka's works describe, is a struggle against bureaucratic absurdity—a maze of illogical demands that leaves one powerless, isolated, and in despair. These systems, originally built for efficiency and protection against fraud, often devolve into oppressive structures that alienate and exhaust customers.

While I do not condone violence, such tragedies compel us to confront difficult questions: Why are systems often designed in ways that hinder rather than serve? Why do corporations sometimes prioritize the relentless pursuit of profit at the expense of meaningful service, when the two can and should coexist? And, in the grand scheme, what value does an additional million achieve that the millions already accumulated cannot, especially if it comes at the cost of principles and purpose?

Pratyahara calls on us to withdraw from outdated, stifling practices and instead create systems grounded in efficiency, empathy, and alignment with a higher purpose. A business that fails to evolve risks suffocating not only its customers but also its own future prospects.

The Need for Innovation: In The Innovator's Dilemma, Clayton Christensen explores why successful businesses often stumble: by clinging to outdated technologies and processes, they lose sight of emerging opportunities. These organizations become so focused on serving their existing customers and maximizing short-term gains that they fail to notice disruptive innovations. These innovations, often simpler and more affordable, may initially appeal only to niche markets or underserved customers. However, over time, they improve and ultimately redefine entire industries, leaving traditional players struggling to catch up. Progress, therefore, often requires businesses to let go of legacy systems and outdated strategies that no longer serve their purpose. By doing so, they create space for forward-thinking innovation, adaptability, and sustained growth in an ever-changing market landscape.

It is often easy to generate new ideas, but the real challenge lies in letting go of what worked in the past—what brought success just a few years ago may soon become obsolete. Similarly, as Marshall Goldsmith emphasizes in *What Got You Here Won't Get You There*, the very strategies and behaviors that once drove success can turn into barriers to future growth. To remain relevant in an ever-evolving environment, leaders must have the courage to abandon outdated practices and develop adaptive skills and forward-looking strategies.

Escalating Commitment and Letting Go: One of the greatest risks business leaders face in this context is the trap of Escalating Commitment. It is a cognitive bias where individuals persist in a failing course of action despite clear evidence that it is not working. Ironically, highly successful individuals are often the most susceptible to this trap. Their fear of admitting failure, especially to themselves, makes it difficult to let go. However, this is where the profound difference between letting go and giving up becomes critical. Letting go, as Pratyahara suggests, is an intentional and strategic act, while giving up is a surrender to defeat. Escalating Commitment, if left unchecked, can result in substantial losses of time, money, and resources. Pratyahara is not about surrendering or giving up; it is about intentionally letting go of what no longer supports the greater purpose.

The Hardest Pratyahara: Toxic Relationships

The hardest part of Pratyahara lies in withdrawing from unproductive or toxic relationships—a challenging but essential practice. In business, this means identifying customers, employees, investors or even co-founders who drain resources, disrupt harmony, or clash with the organization's purpose. Toxic relationships, whether personal or professional, sap emotional and mental energy that could otherwise fuel growth and progress. Interestingly, research reveals that 20% of customers typically consume 80% of resources, and an even smaller subset—just 4% (20% of the 20%)—can account for as much as 64% (80% of the 80%). Although it may seem counterintuitive, quickly identifying and letting go of these 4% of customers is crucial for maintaining focus and maximizing efficiency. No customer or employee, however crucial they might seem at the moment, is irreplaceable. It requires the determination of Pratyahara to let them go, ensuring resources are directed toward relationships that genuinely support the organization's mission.

Bob Pritchett, in *Fire Someone Today: And Other Surprising Tactics for Making Your Business a Success*, emphasizes the importance of parting ways with customers or team members who do not align with the vision or values of the business. By doing so, organizations preserve focus, foster efficiency, and create space for relationships that propel them forward rather than hold them back. It is a bold step, but one that is necessary for lasting success.

Personal Relationships: A Greater Challenge

The challenge of practicing Pratyahara becomes even more pronounced in personal relationships, where emotions, shared history, and deep connections create a complex web. Unfulfilled or toxic relationships often become significant barriers to personal and professional growth. Such relationships not only sap energy but also generate mental distractions that cloud clarity and focus. In these situations, the principles of Yama, particularly Ahimsa (non-violence), play a vital role. If the decision to withdraw from a relationship is fueled by revenge or the desire to settle a score, it breaches the principle of non-violence, even when no physical harm is involved. Conversely, when the intent is guided by the greater good—be it the health of an organization or the well-being of those involved—it aligns with the essence of Pratyahara.

The Courage to Act: Pratyahara requires introspection, a clear purpose, and the courage to act. This applies not only to personal relationships but also to professional ones. When undertaking Pratyahara, the overwhelming consideration should be the eventual benefit of the individual subjected to it. It involves making tough choices that prioritize the greater good while ensuring that individuals are not rejected or disregarded.

When applied to thoughts, Pratyahara demands grit and resilience, requiring us to confront and manage our own mind and emotions. When applied to processes, it necessitates determination and focus, involving the streamlining and optimization of systems and workflows. And when applied to technology, it calls for financial wisdom and discernment, guiding informed decisions about investments and resource allocation.

In essence, Pratyahara embodies mindful action and conscious choice. It is the art of discerning when to engage and when to withdraw, when to act and when to observe merely as a *Drishta* (witness). Through the practice of Pratyahara, we cultivate deeper self-awareness, inner peace, and a clear sense of purpose, enriching both our personal and professional lives.

Practical Approach to Pratyahara

Pratyahara, the practice of withdrawing from distractions to turn inward, may appear abstract but can be seamlessly integrated into daily life with structured methods. Below are some practical strategies:

1. **Daily Digital Detox (15–30 minutes)**
   - Why: Screens dominate our waking hours, often leaving the mind overstimulated and unable to focus.
   - How: Dedicate a specific time daily to disconnect entirely from digital devices. Replace scrolling with activities like journaling, walking, or mindful breathing.

- Benefit: Enhances mental clarity, reduces overstimulation, and fosters deeper creativity by creating mental "white space."

2. **Scheduled Mindfulness Breaks (5 minutes, Twice Daily)**
   - Why: The constant influx of external stimuli reduces mental bandwidth and focus.
   - How: Pause during work hours for brief mindfulness sessions. Close your eyes, breathe deeply, and reset your mental state without engaging with external distractions.
   - Benefit: Promotes the shift from high-stress beta waves, associated with active problem-solving and mental clutter, to calming alpha waves, which enhance relaxation and creativity, fostering clarity for effective decision-making.

3. **Silent Mornings (Once a Week)**
   - Why: Silence provides a reprieve from the noise of daily life, offering a rare opportunity to recalibrate.
   - How: Dedicate one morning weekly to quietude—eschew conversations, news, and social media in favor of slow, intentional activities.
   - Benefit: Cultivates emotional stability and enhances focus, providing a platform for introspection and better self-awareness.

4. **Monthly "Subtraction" Exercise**
   - Why: Habits, tasks, and processes that no longer serve us often weigh us down without notice.

- How: Identify a habit, process, or even possession that feels redundant or draining. Actively replace it with something meaningful or eliminate it altogether.
- Benefit: Simplifies life by reducing unnecessary cognitive load, clearing space for priorities that truly matter.

5. **Pratyahara Conferences for Organizations (Every 6 months)**
   - Why: Businesses often carry inefficiencies in legacy systems or redundant relationships that hinder growth.
   - How: Host a meeting to gather employee input on processes, meetings, or practices that can be removed. Similarly, evaluate unproductive customer or partner relationships.
   - Benefit: Fosters innovation by freeing resources for new opportunities and ensuring operations stay true to core objectives.

6. **Relationships Audit (Every year)**
   - Why: Relationships that no longer reflect one's values or goals can drain emotional and professional energy.
   - How: Once a year, evaluate personal and professional connections. Identify those that drain energy or hinder mutual growth, and take steps to distance yourself or recalibrate the relationship.
   - Benefit: Strengthens focus and emotional resilience by nurturing connections that add value while consciously letting go of those that detract.

By embedding these small, intentional practices into your routine, Pratyahara becomes a tangible and transformative tool for success. It is to remind us that true progress lies not in relentless accumulation but in purposeful subtraction. After all, the bulb wasn't created by constantly adding new features to candles—it was born by a determination to let them go.

Dharana
(Concentration)

Most of us remember using a magnifying glass as children to focus sunlight and burn paper—a vivid demonstration of the power of concentrated energy. This simple act required the right amount of sunlight, a steady hand, and the correct distance between the glass and the paper—all working together to create unwavering focus. In yoga, Dharana (*dha-run-aa*), the sixth limb of Ashtanga Yoga, embodies this principle of concentration. It involves holding the mind steady on a single point or thought, excluding all distractions. This is a deliberate act of mental control, aiming to focus the mind on one thing at a time.

In many ways, Dharana is the first step toward Dhyana (meditation), where the goal is not to just think but to focus intensely and without interruption on one single object, thought, or intention. In a business context, Dharana translates to focusing your energy and attention on a few key objectives—goals, strategies, or a company's mission—while resisting the temptation to spread your energy across a multitude of trivial tasks or distractions. This focused attention creates clarity and allows us to drive towards our most important goals.

The Power of Focus

Focus is a precious commodity in today's world, where distractions are abundant at every turn—be it through constant social media updates, incessant notifications, or endless meetings. These distractions can easily derail us from our core goals, leading to fragmented efforts and diluted results. Dharana, the practice of concentrating the mind and energy, becomes essential to overcoming these distractions. By embracing the art of focus, we can channel our resources into the most meaningful tasks that move the needle on our long-term vision.

Steve Jobs famously said, "Focusing is about saying no." This insight highlights the power of focusing on fewer things with greater intensity, rather than scattering attention across numerous tasks. Apple's success was built on this principle—Jobs and his team concentrated on just a few iconic products, such as the iPhone and MacBook, allowing them to innovate and dominate the market. Similarly, Warren Buffett emphasized that "really successful people say no to almost everything." Buffett's approach underscores the importance of focus and the discipline to say no to distractions and opportunities that do not align with your primary goals. Businesses that prioritize their focus on what truly matters are more likely to achieve their desired outcomes, as they are not sidetracked by competing priorities.

Focused Success in Action

Google's early success exemplifies the power of focus. By concentrating all its efforts on search technology and refining its algorithm, Google revolutionized the way people accessed information. Once it dominated search, Google leveraged its success to branch into cloud computing, AI, and digital advertising. Tesla provides another example of Dharana in practice. With its unwavering commitment to sustainable energy and electric vehicles, Tesla has transformed the automotive industry. From the very beginning, the company channeled its resources into pushing the boundaries of electric mobility, which has led to groundbreaking innovations in vehicle performance and energy storage solutions. Tesla's example demonstrates how concentrated focus on a singular mission can disrupt entire industries and create long-term value for both the company and society.

Theory of Constraints: A Focused Approach to Problem-Solving

The Theory of Constraints, introduced by Dr. Eliyahu M. Goldratt in his book *The Goal*, aligns perfectly with the principles of Dharana by emphasizing the importance of focusing on one constraint at a time. This theory suggests that any system has a single bottleneck or constraint that limits its overall performance. The key to improving the system is to identify that constraint, maximize its output, and ensure that all other processes are aligned to support it. Once the constraint is addressed, the focus shifts to the next bottleneck.

Similar to Dharana, which encourages focusing the mind on one object or thought, the Theory of Constraints stresses the power of concentrated effort in addressing specific challenges. By focusing on the most critical issue at any given time, businesses can increase efficiency, reduce waste, and improve their overall performance. The application of this focused approach can bring about dramatic improvements in productivity and problem-solving across the entire organization.

Prioritizing Focus: Deep Work and The One Thing

In his book *Deep Work*, Cal Newport defines "deep work" as the act of immersing oneself in cognitively demanding tasks without interruption. Newport argues that this type of work not only boosts productivity but also fosters creativity and innovation. Newport advocates for structured practices like time-blocking, where specific periods of the day are dedicated solely to deep work, free from interruptions. This technique aligns closely with the principles of Dharana, as both involve committing time and mental energy to focus on one task or objective without outside distractions. By minimizing what he calls "shallow work"—repetitive, low-value tasks that are easy to replicate—and prioritizing deep work, we can dedicate our energy to high-impact activities that drive progress, yield superior results, and create a more meaningful impact.

The key concept from Gary Keller and Jay Papasan's book, *The One Thing*, is to identify and prioritize the single most impactful task. By asking the question, "What's the ONE Thing you can do such that by doing it everything else will be easier or unnecessary?", businesses can simplify their approach and concentrate efforts on what truly matters. This core task then becomes the focal point, streamlining all other activities and ensuring they align with the primary goal. Ultimately, this method of prioritization allows businesses to optimize their resources and achieve greater success.

When applied together, the principles from *Deep Work* and *The One Thing* provide a comprehensive approach to success. By fostering a culture of focus, clarity, and prioritization, we can ensure that every action aligns with our strategic goals. Practicing Dharana transforms focus into a powerful competitive advantage, driving innovation, productivity, and sustainable growth.

Practical Approach to Dharana

The sixth limb of yoga, Dharana serves as the gateway to deeper meditation (Dhyana) and self-realization (Samadhi). Dharana can be practiced as a way to cultivate sustained focus, eliminate distractions, and enhance mental clarity. Here's how to integrate Dharana into your routine:

1. **The Single-Task Rule (Daily Practice)**
   - Why: Multitasking divides attention and reduces efficiency.
   - How: Commit to completing one task at a time. Use tools like the Pomodoro Technique (25-minute focus intervals followed by a 5-minute break) to train your brain to concentrate on one activity without interruption.
   - Benefit: Enhances productivity, reduces errors, and strengthens your ability to focus over time.
2. **Focus Anchors (5-10 Minutes Daily)**
   - Why: The mind tends to wander, especially in the face of multiple stimuli.
   - How: Choose an anchor such as your breath, mild music, a mantra, or a specific object (like a candle flame). Set a timer for 5-10 minutes and focus solely on this anchor, gently bringing your attention back whenever it drifts.
   - Benefit: Trains the mind to remain present and cultivates the discipline of returning to the task at hand.

3. **Visualization Exercises (10 Minutes Daily)**
   - Why: Visualization helps build mental clarity and strengthens cognitive focus.
   - How: Close your eyes and visualize a specific goal, project, or ideal outcome in vivid detail. Focus on the colors, sounds, and sensations associated with this vision. Let your concentration immerse you in the experience.
   - Benefit: Enhances creativity, motivation, and the ability to focus on long-term goals.

4. **Focused Reading or Learning (15-20 Minutes Daily)**
   - Why: Concentrated reading or learning challenges the brain to focus on absorbing information without distraction.
   - How: Dedicate time each day to reading a book or learning a new skill without interruptions. Avoid skimming or multitasking—immerse yourself fully in the material. Use technology like Duolingo if you are learning a language.
   - Benefit: Improves mental discipline, comprehension, and the ability to sustain attention.

5. **Time-Boxing for Deep Work (1-2 Hours Weekly)**
   - Why: Prolonged focus is essential for tackling complex tasks or creative projects.
   - How: Schedule specific blocks of time for uninterrupted work on high-priority tasks. Communicate this boundary to colleagues to minimize interruptions.

- Benefit: Enhances problem-solving skills, fosters innovation, and builds mental endurance.

6. **Soundscapes for Focus (Daily Use)**
   - Why: The right auditory environment can support concentration.
   - How: Use binaural beats, white noise, or instrumental music to create a soundscape that promotes focus. Pair this with a designated workspace free from distractions.
   - Benefit: Improves mental clarity and supports sustained attention during demanding tasks.

7. **Reflection Journaling (Evening Practice, 10 Minutes)**
   - Why: Reflecting on focus lapses helps identify patterns and improve concentration.
   - How: At the end of each day, journal about moments when your focus was sharp and when it faltered. Reflect on what caused distractions and how you can manage them better.
   - Benefit: Builds self-awareness and reinforces habits that support Dharana.

8. **Group Focus Activities (Monthly Practice)**
   - Why: Practicing focus in a group setting enhances accountability and discipline.
   - How: Organize a focus group session, where participants work on individual tasks for a set period without speaking or distractions. Share reflections afterward.
   - Benefit: Encourages shared discipline and fosters a culture of concentration within teams.

9. **Dharana for Decision-Making (Situational Practice)**
   - Why: Complex decisions require undivided attention and clarity.
   - How: When faced with a critical decision, withdraw to a quiet space and focus entirely on the issue at hand. Use frameworks like mind-mapping to explore solutions without external distractions.
   - Benefit: Improves decision quality and strengthens strategic thinking.

By incorporating these practices, Dharana becomes a powerful tool for cultivating unwavering focus, enhancing productivity, and navigating the complexities of life with clarity and purpose.

Dhyana
(Meditation)

Dhyana (*dhi-ya-na*), the seventh limb of Ashtanga Yoga, is meditation—a state where concentration evolves into complete absorption. While Dharana (concentration) involves the deliberate, effortful act of directing attention to a single object or thought, Dhyana transcends this effort. As meditation deepens, focus no longer requires active concentration. Instead, the mind enters a state where the object of focus is experienced naturally and seamlessly, without effort. The transition from "effortful focus" to "effortless flow" is at the heart of Dhyana—where concentration matures into complete immersion.

In this state, the meditator no longer struggles to maintain focus; instead, the mind remains effortlessly engaged, allowing distractions to dissolve naturally. Time disappears, and the individual becomes fully absorbed in the present moment. This is the state where the mind reaches its highest potential, enabling clarity, insight, and awareness. The meditator and the object of meditation become one, and the experience is marked by uninterrupted immersion.

Dhyana and Spirituality

Dhyana is not merely a mental exercise; it is also a deeply spiritual practice. The *Bhagavad Gita*, a timeless scripture, extensively discusses the importance of meditation. In Chapter 6.19, Lord Krishna compares the focused mind in meditation to a steady flame in a windless place: *"As a lamp in a windless place does not flicker, so is a yogi whose mind is controlled, remaining steady in meditation on the Self."* This verse captures the essence of Dhyana—calm, unwavering focus that brings stability and self-awareness.

Lord Krishna also explains in Chapter 6.7, *"The yogi who has attained self-mastery, whose mind is calm, who is free from dualities, and who sees the same in all beings, remains steadfast in meditation."* This focus on the self and detachment from external distractions is at the heart of Dhyana, facilitating the union between the individual self and the higher self.

Dhyana allows us to transcend worldly concerns, creating a space for deeper understanding and connection to the divine. This spiritual aspect of meditation invites inner peace, self-realization, and a profound sense of unity with the universe.

Dynamic Meditation

While traditional meditation often involves stillness, the concept of dynamic meditation expands the practice to include movement, sound, and active expression. Popularized by spiritual leaders like Osho, dynamic meditation emphasizes that meditation is not limited to quiet contemplation. Instead, it can be active and engaging, involving the body and mind simultaneously. This dynamic approach perfectly complements the philosophy of Dhyana, where the self merges with the action at hand.

For example, singing can be a form of dynamic meditation (and I have yet to come across someone who does not sing, at least in the bathroom). Similarly, sporting activities as simple as playing ping-pong can exemplify dynamic meditation. In ping-pong, the player must initially concentrate fully on the tiny ball, and the effortful focus quickly transitions into effortless flow. This immersion in the present moment is not just about physical fitness; it is a form of mindfulness that can be practiced daily.

Demanding activities like marathons, triathlons, and mountain climbing also offer examples of dynamic meditation. These pursuits require total focus, a balance between skill and challenge, and the ability to remain fully present. Whether through physical exertion or mental resilience, these activities exemplify Dhyana in action, with participants often entering a flow state that fosters clarity, creativity, and purpose. Business leaders who engage in such endeavors can bring the same focused energy and mindfulness at work, enhancing their problem-solving abilities and decision-making.

Modern Methods

The modern world has seen a shift toward accessible methods for practicing meditation, making Dhyana more relatable to individuals seeking mindfulness in the hustle and bustle of daily life. Apps like *Headspace* and *Calm* offer guided meditations and mindfulness exercises that introduce users to the benefits of meditation, including reducing stress and improving mental clarity. Despite their simplicity, these practices, derived from traditional methods, enable individuals to calm their busy minds and find stability amidst a world of distractions.

Alongside these tools, books like *Flow: The Psychology of Optimal Experience* by Mihaly Csikszentmihalyi provide profound insight into how individuals can achieve deep immersion in tasks. Csikszentmihalyi defines flow as a state in which a person becomes fully absorbed in an activity, achieving a balance between the level of challenge and their skill. In this state, individuals lose track of time and self-consciousness, becoming entirely engaged with the task at hand. Csikszentmihalyi highlights that flow occurs when the activity provides clear goals, immediate feedback, and a sense of control, allowing people to operate at their fullest potential. This state of immersion parallels Dhyana, where the mind is fully absorbed in the object of meditation, and distractions fade away.

Modern professionals, especially leaders, experience this flow state in high-stakes situations, whether it's solving complex problems, leading teams through uncertainty, or making quick decisions under pressure. The balance between skill and challenge that creates flow can also be seen in the intense focus required by athletes, musicians, or even doctors performing surgeries. Csikszentmihalyi argues that cultivating flow in everyday life not only enhances personal fulfillment but also promotes productivity, creativity, and a sense of accomplishment. Just as in Dhyana, where meditation helps maintain focus and clarity, flow allows professionals to perform at their highest level, bringing together focus, skill, and mindfulness to achieve optimal outcomes.

By integrating mindfulness into both work and daily life, we can create a more intentional approach to the demands of modern living. Whether through apps or physical activities that induce flow, modern methods of meditation help cultivate the presence and focus central to Dhyana. This practice, whether through traditional meditation, dynamic exercises, or modern tools, enables us to transcend distractions, enhance awareness, and connect with a higher purpose. By making meditation a part of daily life, we can achieve a profound state of focus and clarity, fostering personal growth and improving leadership, decision-making, and creativity in both personal and professional spheres.

Practical Approach to Dhyana

1. Daily Micro-Meditations (5–10 minutes)

Why: Short meditation sessions are easier to sustain, reducing stress and increasing focus over time.

How: Dedicate 5–10 minutes each morning before starting work, or in the evening to wind down. Focus on your breath, a mantra, or even ambient sounds. Don't worry if stray thoughts emerge—simply acknowledge them and return to your focus. For beginners, guided meditation apps like Headspace or Calm provide structure to help ease into the practice.

Benefit: Improves emotional resilience, heightens focus, and cultivates inner calm throughout the day.

2. Mindful Transitions (1–2 minutes)

Why: Fast-paced schedules often leave little time to reset between tasks.

How: Use brief moments between tasks to pause, close your eyes, and take deep breaths. Shift from one activity to another with mindfulness, instead of rushing. For instance, before a meeting, ask everyone to engage in one minute of silent stillness with closed eyes to recenter. Some organizations introduce a brief "Om" chant before meetings to prepare the team mentally and emotionally.

Benefit: Enhances clarity, reduces overwhelm, and allows for more effective transitions between tasks.

3. **Group Meditation Sessions (Weekly or Monthly)**

Why: Collective meditation fosters team unity and shared clarity.

How: Organize a 15–20 minute group meditation at work or in community gatherings. This can include simple breathing exercises or a silent meditation practice led by a facilitator. It serves as a powerful team-building exercise, especially when done consistently.

Benefit: Strengthens team cohesion, reduces workplace stress, and nurtures a culture of mindfulness.

4. **Silent Evenings**

Why: Extended periods of quiet allow the mind to unwind and transition into deeper meditative states.

How: Dedicate one evening each week to silence, preferably during the workweek. Avoid conversations, media, and even reading. Instead, engage in mindful activities like slow walking, journaling, or simply sitting in stillness.

Benefit: Facilitates deeper self-reflection and strengthens the ability to maintain sustained focus.

5. Immersive Retreats (Annually or Quarterly)

Why: Meditation retreats offer an opportunity for profound immersion in Dhyana, away from daily distractions.

How: Attend a silent retreat or yoga workshop, even for a weekend. Many organizations host retreats focused on mindfulness and emotional detoxification.

Benefit: Provides mental rejuvenation, offers a reset from routine, and encourages insights into personal growth and aspirations.

PART FOUR

The OUTCOME.

"Success is not the key to happiness. Happiness is the key to success. If you love what you are doing, you will be successful."

— Albert Schweitzer

Samadhi
The Pinnacle of Business Yoga

Samadhi, the eighth and ultimate limb of Ashtanga Yoga, represents unity and transcendence. Derived from the Sanskrit words *Sama* (equanimity) and *Dhi* (awareness), it signifies a state where the mind achieves complete harmony, merging seamlessly with its focus. In this state, all distractions dissolve, and existence itself becomes an act of profound awareness. Samadhi is not an abstract spiritual ideal; it is the culmination of human potential, where purpose, action, and vision converge in perfect unison.

For each of the previous limbs of Ashtanga Yoga, I have provided practical approaches to help you incorporate their essence into your business and personal life. Samadhi, however, is unique. It is not something you do—it is something that happens to you. It is not a task you undertake—it is an experience that unfolds naturally. Like a sunrise that unfolds effortlessly when the conditions are right, Samadhi arises naturally when the journey through the previous limbs prepares you for this ultimate state. You cannot force or control it; you can only allow it.

Human Beings and the Essence of Being

Samadhi resonates with the term *human being*. Unlike other species defined by action—hunting, building, surviving—humans possess a unique capacity for stillness, for existing in a state of pure being. This capacity, reflected in our language, highlights an inherent potential to transcend the cycle of constant action and embrace the unity of existence. Samadhi epitomizes this capacity, allowing us to move beyond doing and into the profound truth of being.

Artists, musicians, and athletes often exemplify this state through their work. When a musician performs with total immersion or an athlete enters the elusive "zone," their craft becomes an extension of their very essence. These moments of peak performance arise not from effort but from flow, where the distinction between the person and the act disappears. Similarly, visual artists describe moments when creativity seems to flow through them rather than from them, as though they are vessels for a greater force. These states are windows into Samadhi—effortless unity between intention and expression.

I am intrigued by some doctors in India with such exceptionally intensive schedules that one might wonder what the purpose of their work is if they cannot find time to live life. But over time, I realized that for these doctors, their work *is* life. The joy and satisfaction they derive from saving lives and making a difference is a reward that no material incentive could ever offer. In these cases, the work itself becomes a profound expression of purpose, embodying the essence of Samadhi, where their calling transcends mere tasks and becomes a true extension of their being.

Purpose-driven entrepreneurs experience a similar phenomenon. For them, work is not a task but a calling—a natural extension of their identity and purpose. They find joy and fulfillment in their endeavors, viewing their businesses not just as profit-generating entities but as vehicles for impact and coherence with their values. This synergy enables them to operate seamlessly, navigating challenges with a sense of clarity and purpose. The problem is that their teams do not share the same excitement as they do. Many entrepreneurs mistakenly assume that their teams have the same dreams as they do, when in fact fostering shared vision requires intentional leadership and deliberate culture-building.

Ikigai and Wu Wei

Two profound philosophies, Ikigai and Wu Wei, gel closely with the essence of Samadhi, offering insights into achieving harmony and flow both personally and within organizations.

Ikigai, a Japanese concept, represents the convergence of:

- What you love: Passion and joy that inspire you.
- What you are good at: Skills and abilities honed over time.

- What the world needs: A purpose that benefits others.
- What you can be paid for: Viability in delivering value.

At the heart of these intersections lies Ikigai—the reason for being. For businesses, discovering their Ikigai fosters coherence between internal values and external demands, creating a harmonious flow where profit becomes an outcome, not the sole objective. Such organizations inspire purpose among stakeholders—customers, employees, suppliers and communities—while cultivating loyalty and innovation. Leaders who embrace Ikigai continually adapt, ensuring that their mission evolves with the changing world.

Wu Wei, a Taoist principle, translates to "effortless action". Often misunderstood as passivity, Wu Wei represents acting in harmony with the natural flow of life, responding to situations with clarity and without resistance. In business, this translates to focusing on simplicity, timing, and authenticity. Leaders practicing Wu Wei understand when to act and when to allow things to unfold naturally, fostering environments of creativity and efficiency without unnecessary pressure or micromanagement.

Ikigai provides the foundation for purpose, while Wu Wei ensures that action flows naturally from that foundation. Together, they guide businesses toward a state of effortlessness, paving the way for the ultimate realization of Samadhi, where innovation, impact, and fulfillment arise seamlessly as a unified whole.

Work as Life: Redefining Balance

The modern narrative of work-life balance often implies a separation that, in reality, does not exist. Work, when infused with purpose, becomes an integral part of life. Just as breathing or sleeping is a natural expression of existence, so too is work. The need for balance only arises when work feels disconnected from who we are. In Samadhi, the boundaries between work and life dissolve. Work becomes an expression of life's purpose—an effortless flow rather than a burdensome obligation.

David J. McNeff, in his book *The Work-Life Balance Myth: Rethinking Your Optimal Balance for Success*, challenges the conventional idea of work-life balance. He introduces the "Seven Slices" method, which views life as interconnected aspects rather than opposing domains. According to McNeff, these "Seven Slices"—family, professional life, personal life, physical health, intellectual pursuits, emotional well-being, and spiritual growth—are all vital components of a person's existence. Each slice must be nurtured and served, as fulfilling these needs in turn supports us. This holistic approach helps individuals achieve a fulfilling and sustainable life by seeing life as a whole, rather than compartmentalized segments that need to be balanced against each other.

Similarly, Matthew Kelly critiques the pursuit of work-life balance in his book *Off Balance: Getting Beyond the*

Work-Life Balance Myth to Personal and Professional Satisfaction. Kelly argues that the idea of a perfect balance is misleading and that true satisfaction lies in integrating work with other aspects of life. He proposes that instead of striving for balance, we should focus on overall satisfaction—achieved when all areas of life are aligned with our values and purpose. By focusing on satisfaction over balance, Kelly encourages a mindset that treats life's various aspects as interconnected, where personal and professional fulfillment are intertwined. Like Samadhi, Kelly's approach promotes the idea that work and life should flow seamlessly, creating a sense of joy and fulfillment rather than stress and division.

Humans Are Not Resources

When we define something as a resource, we inherently limit its potential. A resource, by definition, has a fixed or defined output. Think of how a machine operates—when it is used for a specific purpose, it performs a set function and delivers an expected result. However, human potential is far from limited in this way. Humans possess limitless creativity, innovation, and the capacity for growth—qualities that a static "resource" cannot embody. When we refer to someone as a "resource," we reduce their value to merely an input-output process, which is fundamentally limiting.

Think about how you would never call your business partner or co-founder a "resource." They are partners in progress, co-creators of a shared vision. If we genuinely consider our employees as partners, the first step is to stop calling them resources. This is not just a semantic shift; it is a mindset change that acknowledges the immense potential they bring to the table. True leadership is not about making people believe in you—it is about helping them believe in themselves and empowering them to unlock their full potential.

Achieving Samadhi in business requires aligning employees with the organization's mission. It is about creating an environment where individuals not only see the value in their roles but also feel deeply connected to the larger purpose of the company. When employees are treated as partners, not as resources, workplaces transform into ecosystems of inspiration and fulfillment. The key is to foster a culture where people can bring their whole selves to work, where creativity is encouraged, and where everyone feels their contributions are meaningful.

The term "human resources," popularized during the Industrial Revolution, framed people as interchangeable components in a production system—a mechanistic approach that does not resonate in today's knowledge-driven economy. This outdated perspective stifles individuality and creativity, which are essential to modern businesses. Treating employees as mere resources dehumanizes them, undervaluing their creativity, emotional intelligence, and the complex, evolving skill sets they bring. Today, businesses thrive when they nurture individuality, foster creativity, and align roles with employees' intrinsic strengths. When employees are seen as partners, they feel empowered to contribute their best work, and the organization benefits from an environment that nurtures growth and innovation.

Samadhi: The Ultimate Expression of Unity

In writing this book, I explored the deeper purpose that connects us all—both as individuals and as businesses. Through numerous conversations and reflections, five universal themes emerged:

1. The desire for personal growth—a yearning to continually learn, evolve, and reach our fullest potential.
2. The strength found in building relationships—fostering connections that nurture love, trust, and mutual support.
3. The fulfillment of making a difference—leaving a positive impact on the world, no matter how small or large.
4. The pursuit of joy—finding happiness in life's simple pleasures and embracing moments of gratitude.
5. The quest for spiritual enlightenment—seeking a deeper understanding of ourselves and our place in the universe.

The essence of Samadhi is a state of being where purpose and action are inseparable, where we recognize that we are, and have always been, part of a greater whole. It transcends individual beliefs and circumstances, pointing us toward a life lived in harmony—with ourselves, with others, and with the world around us. Work and life are not separate realms to be balanced but inseparable facets of a unified existence. When businesses embrace this truth, they transcend their role as mere economic engines to become catalysts for harmony. They create environments where individuals derive meaning from their contributions, where innovation emerges effortlessly, and where collective growth fosters individual fulfillment. By nurturing these spaces, businesses elevate both the Standard of Living and the Standard of Life, enabling people to thrive as a cohesive part of the larger whole.

Let *Business Yoga* remind us that true success lies not in what we achieve, but in how deeply we live, connect, and embrace the interconnectedness of a greater whole.

OM!

***

<u>Epilogue</u>
Why Business Yoga?

Long before the writing of *Business Yoga* began, a recurring question lingered in my mind: Why does work feel like a burden to so many? And yet, for a select few, it seems to be an extension of life's purpose. Whenever visitors came to our facilities, especially Westerners, their comments often followed a familiar pattern: "Everyone here seems so joyful." Some even spoke of sensing a positive aura. These observations intrigued me.

In conversations with captivated audiences, I often shared my thoughts on the principles of yoga. On several occasions, I was invited to speak about the philosophy that guided my business practices. The term *Business Yoga* was not something I set out to formalize; it was one I spontaneously coined to capture what I saw as the essence of three profound paths: Gyan, Karma, and Bhakti Yoga:

- Gyan Yoga emphasizes understanding and wisdom— an unending journey of questioning, seeking, and exploring.

- Karma Yoga elevates action, urging us to perform our duties selflessly and with mindfulness, recognizing that every deed contributes to the larger fabric of existence.
- Bhakti Yoga is the yoga of devotion, not only in worship but also in loving what you do and offering it unconditionally to the greater good.

Each of these paths has the depth to fill countless volumes, and yet what I have attempted here is merely to scratch the surface, offering practical applications for modern business and leadership.

Yoga's wisdom has been passed down orally for thousands of years, encapsulated into 196 sutras by the sage Maharshi Patanjali in the 2nd century BCE. While my book touches on many aspects of this philosophy, I make no pretense of being an authority. I am simply a practitioner who has applied some basic principles of yoga to the business world with practical results.

I hope this book serves as an invitation for business leaders to explore what the universe has to offer when approached with balance, mindfulness, and purpose. Throughout the book, you will find references to modern business literature by accomplished luminaries, which, knowingly or unknowingly, echo ancient wisdom in their own ways.

Yoga is fundamentally about harmonizing opposites—balancing the seven chakras, the Ida and Pingala energy channels, and even the five basic elements, or Panchmahabhootas. I have resisted the temptation to delve deeply into these concepts, but I have offered glimpses in the appendix, such as a brief synopsis of balancing the five elements.

Let me be clear: *Business Yoga* is not a spiritual or religious text. It is a practical guide. It acknowledges that money, far from being antithetical to purpose, is an essential aspect of life. The principles discussed in this book are meant to help you harmonize the pursuit of material success with a deeper sense of fulfillment and joy.

I believe in the power of community, or *Sangha*. The Sangha is not just a group of people; it is a collective force of wisdom, guidance, and shared purpose. Similarly, I hope this book inspires you to form your own Sanghas—groups where ideas from *Business Yoga* can be shared, debated, and critically examined.

Take, for instance, the Jain philosophy of *Anekantavada,* which teaches us that multiple truths can coexist. Use this philosophy to challenge and refine the ideas in this book. I am not asking for blind acceptance but for thoughtful engagement.

Business Yoga is an invitation to enjoy your work so much that you never "need" a holiday—you only "want" one. Imagine a world where work is not a chore but an extension of your life's purpose, where business is not just about competition but about collaboration, balance, and collective growth.

In the end, achieving balance in business, just like in Yoga, is a journey. It is about continuous refinement, mindful exploration, and a willingness to adapt to new truths. I hope this book has provided you with not just insights but also the inspiration to reimagine work as a source of joy, purpose, and enduring harmony.

Here's to a future where every workplace radiates joy, every leader embodies purpose, and every action contributes to a greater sense of balance in the world.

Let the journey of *Business Yoga* continue—beyond these pages and into your life.

****

Acknowledgements

Never before have I owed so much to so many! To all of you, I am bound to forget a few—but without your contributions, this journey would not have been possible.

Writing a book on such esoteric concepts, while maintaining brevity, was a challenge unlike any I have faced before. It reminded me of what my daughter, Avantika, often says, quoting Mark Twain: "If I had more time, I would have written a shorter letter." At first, this seemed counterintuitive, but as I immersed myself in *Business Yoga*, I realized that simplicity often requires the greatest effort.

To my late father, who staked everything to allow me to venture into the world of business. Little did I know the impact of his act of pledging all his savings as collateral to secure the bank loan. To my mother, who continues to be the unwavering emotional anchor in my life. To my family—Avantika, Sanchit, and Harshvardhan—your love, support, and intellectual curiosity have been my bedrock. Avantika's sharp insights were invaluable, pushing me to refine the manuscript, streamline the history of business, include engaging anecdotes, elaborate on the longevity of business in comparison to the human lifespan, and, most importantly, to leave space for unanswered questions that would provoke deeper thinking in readers.

I am deeply grateful to my son, Harshvardhan, Founder of V-Comply.com, whose ceaseless curiosity about the book's progress kept me on my toes. To my son-in-law, Sanchit Jain, whose thoughtful questions about the book's concepts guided me to refine my thoughts and redraft several sections, I owe much of the clarity in these pages.

To the countless workers at Kariwala Industries Ltd., whose joy, dedication, and embodiment of *Business Yoga* continue to inspire not only me but the many visitors to our facilities, I owe my deepest gratitude. Without their commitment, this book would never have seen the light of day.

A heartfelt thanks to my dear friend Hans Geels, who not only graciously wrote the foreword but also lives and breathes the principles of *Business Yoga* in both his personal and professional life at Dille & Kamille in Holland.

I am also deeply grateful to my colleagues—Anand Sureka, Manish Todi, Ranjit Singh, Rudradeep Sinha, Rajrupa Dutta, Adena Sengupta, and Veena Das—whose feedback on the manuscript and daily practice of *Business Yoga* helped ensure that we live what we teach. Payal Sharma's meticulous work in collating the bibliography, and Rohan Singh's tireless coordination with the publishers, played crucial roles in making this book what it is.

A special mention to Bajrang Banthia, Prasad Ramakrishnan, and Hiten Udani, my colleagues on the board of Kariwala Industries. They read the manuscript, and like a lighthouse in the storm, guided me through challenging decisions, ensuring we navigated without running the ship aground.

I owe much to Parthasarathy Ranganathan, Executive Director at Morgan Stanley, not only for his valuable feedback but also for his articles, which sharpened this book and broadened its horizons.

Alok Maheshwary, my childhood friend, reviewed the manuscript in the midst of his busy schedule as Managing Director at State Street. His brilliant suggestion to include a ready reckoner, distilling the core concepts of *Business Yoga*, and his advice on writing practical approaches for each limb of Yoga, have made a profound impact on the book. His framing of spirituality as an operating system—a principle we uphold at Kariwala Industries Ltd.—has been transformative.

Lynn Scheurell, author of *Heal the Chakras of Your Business: Adapt Ancient Wellness Systems for the Wealth of Your Business Today*, deserves my deepest thanks for her encouraging blurb and thoughtful reading of the manuscript. Similarly, I am grateful to Robert Purse and Graham Smedley, co-authors of my first book *People: The Heart of*

Good Governance, whose encouragement to pursue this project showed me that even a small part of a larger vision can make an enormous impact.

Dr. K. Rangarajan, Director at the Indian Institute of Foreign Trade, deserves special mention for not only providing insightful feedback but also suggesting that this book has the potential to be a textbook for business schools.

Professors Jesper Sorensen and Baba Shiv from Stanford University were instrumental in helping me connect the teachings from the Stanford Seed Transformation Program to the principles of *Business Yoga*. Their profound influence shaped much of what this book represents.

I owe a great deal to Darius Teter, Executive Director at Stanford Seed, whose insights provided the most comprehensive summary of the core principles underpinning this book. Not only did Darius offer a valuable perspective from the Western world, but his deep understanding, honed at the heart of business education at Stanford University, helped me refine my ideas and sharpen the focus of the book.

Sahil Khandwala, Kamna Agarwal, and Raj Shekhar Parcha—fellow members of my Stanford cohort—dedicated time and energy to read the manuscript and provide invaluable feedback. Sahil, with his tireless spirit, continues to inspire me not only as a business leader but as a mountain climber and voracious reader. Raj Shekhar, the founder of

GoApptiv, with his spiritual depth, helped me refine many of the book's concepts, offering suggestions that otherwise might have escaped my attention.

Matteo Borri's influence on the concept of dynamic meditation was transformative. His embodiment of balance—climbing the Alps for the 'weekend rest' and doing triathlons—serves as a perfect example of how one can live the principles of *Business Yoga*.

Govind Beriwal, Shambhu Saraf, and Rajesh Somani, my dear friends, have been steadfast in their exploration of the Bhagavad Gita with me every Saturday. These intellectual exchanges have shaped the foundation of the spiritual principles that underpin *Business Yoga*.

A special mention to Rajesh Nahata, who selflessly stood by me when I began this business and has been a constant source of support.

To Priya Agarwal, my colleague, who designed the cover of this book. She is the finest Mandala artist I know. Her artwork resonates deeply with the principles of *Business Yoga*, and describing its resonance would require pages. Likewise, I am grateful to Vineeta Killa, a friend who was almost like my sounding board, and who selflessly read the manuscript, pointing out repetitions I had inadvertently allowed to seep in.

Rakhi Kapoor's comprehensive feedback has been invaluable. As the only author I personally know who has written 28 best-sellers, her words of encouragement continue to inspire me.

Rahul Shukla, who drives HDFC Bank, deserves my thanks for his review of the manuscript and his words of encouragement.

Rick Levine, the executive director at NAUMD, gave me countless practical tips in writing this book, and his unwavering encouragement helped me stay motivated. Rick also helped me land my first ever podcast.

I am also deeply grateful to Ken DePaul from Universal Studios, whose encouraging words were a source of motivation. His joyful outlook on life and work in the business of joy itself has been an inspiration.

To Alkesh Agarwal, an entrepreneur with profound clarity of thought, thank you for your insights and thoughtful contributions to this process.

To the team of translators, including Chandrashekhar Shrimali—thank you for doing a commendable job in translating this book into Hindi, Bengali, German, French, Spanish, Italian, Japanese, and Dutch. Your efforts have made *Business Yoga* accessible to a global audience.

Finally, I must express my deepest gratitude to Late Shri Shyam Sundar Lohia. His profound lectures on the deeper meanings of the Bhagavad Gita, conveyed in the simplest and most accessible manner, served as the foundation and inspiration for much of the content in this book.

This book is a reflection of all those who have helped shape its journey. Whether named or not, your presence has been felt, and this book belongs as much to you as it does to me.

With deep gratitude,

Anil Kariwala

<u>Appendix – 1</u>
Basic Tenets of the 7 Chakras

Here's a concise table summarizing the basic tenets of the **Seven Chakras**, synopsized as a ready reckoner

Chakra	Business Representation	Core Attributes	Relevance to Business
Muladhara (Root)	Foundation and Stability	Security and Survival	Energizes the foundation of a business, akin to its business model. Stability in resources, cash flow, and purpose to ensure resilience.

Chakra	Business Representation	Core Attributes	Relevance to Business
Swadhisthana (Sacral)	Creativity and Innovation	Emotion and Creativity	Embodies the creative energy needed for innovation, adaptability, and design thinking. Energizes team harmony.
Manipura (Solar Plexus)	Leadership and Drive	Confidence and Power	Energizes leadership styles, decision-making power, and execution strength, crucial for steering businesses.
Anahata (Heart)	Connection and Empathy	Compassion and Love	Energizes customer-centricity, ethical leadership, and fostering relationships with employees, customers, suppliers or society.

Chakra	Business Representation	Core Attributes	Relevance to Business
Vishuddha (Throat)	Communication and Transparency	Truth and Expression	Energizes open communication, honest marketing, and clear leadership to inspire trust and loyalty.
Ajna (Third Eye)	Vision and Intuition	Insight and Clarity	Energizes strategic vision, foresight, and the ability to balance intuition with data-driven decisions.
Sahasrara (Crown)	Purpose and Enlightenment	Awareness and Connection	Embodies the energy to pursue higher goals, such as sustainability, societal impact, and a greater sense of purpose beyond profits.

Appendix – 2
The Energy Channels

This table highlights the dual forces of **Ida and Pingala** in a business setting, emphasizing the importance of balancing intuition and logic for sustainable success.

Aspect	Ida	Pingala
Symbolic Energy	Cooling, nurturing, and introspective	Heating, active, and dynamic
Associated Attributes	Creativity, intuition, emotional intelligence, and reflection	Logic, analysis, strategy, and execution
Business Functions	Energizes long-term vision, creative problem-solving, and empathetic leadership	Energizes goal-setting, task execution, and performance measurement
Decision-Making	Encourages intuitive, human-centered approaches	Drives data-driven, analytical decision-making
Leadership Style	Focused on employee well-being, collaboration, and harmony	Focused on results, efficiency, and achieving targets

Aspect	Ida	Pingala
Balance in Business	Helps to cultivate a compassionate workplace culture	Ensures productivity, competitiveness, and operational excellence
Chakra Connection	Often linked to the **left energy channel** in yogic philosophy (moon energy)	Often linked to the **right energy channel** in yogic philosophy (sun energy)

Appendix – 3
The Attributes of Yoga

Here's a concise table that summarizes the attributes of Ashtanga Yoga that can be used as a ready reckoner:

Limb	Meaning	Focus	Application
Yama	The Principles	Non-violence, truthfulness, non-stealing, non-possessiveness and moderation.	Builds ethical foundations and fosters integrity in personal and professional relationships.
Niyama	Personal Discipline	Self Purification, contentment, self-discipline, self-reflection, and surrender to a higher purpose.	Encourages self-improvement, gratitude, and alignment with personal and organizational goals.

Limb	Meaning	Focus	Application
Asana	Physical Postures	Stability, ease, and body-mind balance.	Enhances physical health and prepares the body for enduring mental and professional challenges.
Pranayama	Breath Control	Regulation of life energy through breath.	Improves focus, energy management, and emotional stability under stress.
Pratyahara	Withdrawal from the unnecessary	Turning inward by detaching from distractions.	Helps leaders and organizations eliminate inefficiencies and focus on purpose-driven strategies.
Dharana	Concentration	Focusing the mind on a single point or task.	Builds focus, enhances productivity, and fosters creative problem-solving.
Dhyana	Meditation	Continuous contemplation or mindfulness.	Promotes clarity, emotional intelligence, and intuitive decision-making.

Limb	Meaning	Focus	Application
Samadhi	Ultimate Absorption or Bliss	A state of unity with one's purpose and surroundings.	This is not what you apply; this is what you achieve by practising Business Yoga. Inspires purpose-driven leadership and integrates work as an integral part of a joyful life.

Appendix – 4
Surya Namaskar

Surya Namaskar, or Sun Salutation, is considered a complete set of yoga asanas and a dynamic practice that invokes the fire element within the body. This sequence prepares the body and mind for deeper yogic practices by activating energy flow and building heat, making it an ideal starting point. It serves as a bridge to the earth element, which is grounded through static asanas that follow.

The following figures demonstrate how Surya Namaskar can be practiced. Each position requires a stay of just 10 seconds, and the set must be performed sequentially, enabling a complete set to be finished in only two minutes:

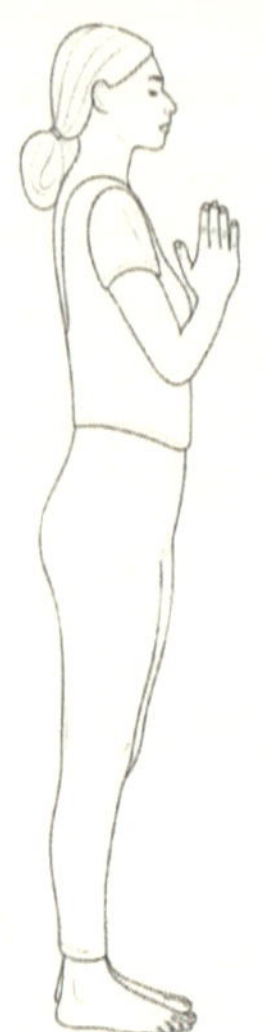

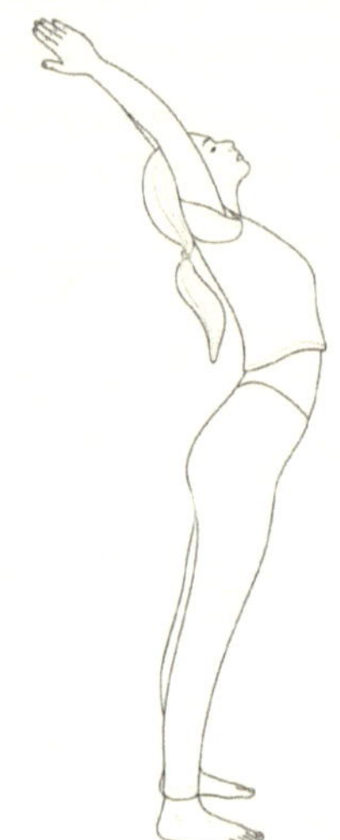

1. Pranamasana

(*Prayer Pose*)

2. Hastauttanasana

(*Raised Arms Pose*)

3. Hastapadasana

(Standing Forward Bend)

4. Ashwa Sanchalanasana

(Equestrian Pose)

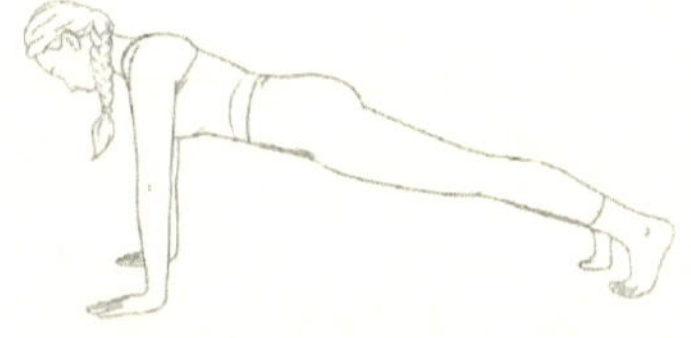

5. Dandasana
(Stick Pose)

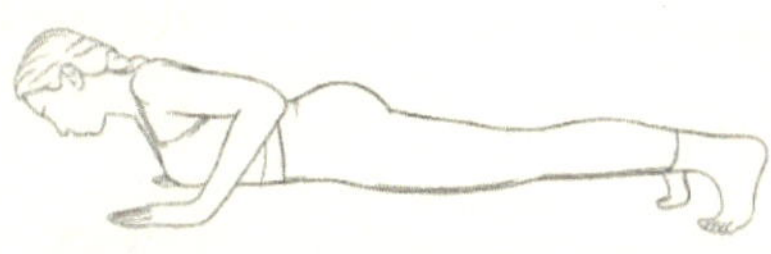

6. Ashtanga Namaskara
(Salute With Eight Parts)

7. Bhujangasana
(*Cobra Pose*)

8. Adho Mukha Svanasana
(*Downward Facing Dog Pose*)

9. Ashwa Sanchalanasana
(*Equestrian Pose*)

10. Hastapadasana
(*Standing Forward Bend*)

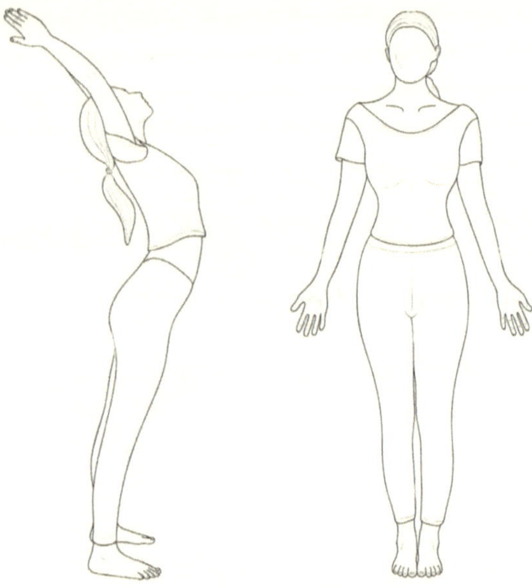

11. Hastauttanasana
(*Raised Arms Pose*)

12. Tadasana
(*Mountain Pose*)

Appendix – 5
A Practical Way for Asanas
(The Postures)

Standing Series

Vrikshasana (Tree Pose):

- Enhances proprioception (bodily awareness), strengthens ankle stability, and engages the core to improve posture. Surprisingly, it may also aid hearing by stabilizing the inner ear.
- Relieves balance issues like vertigo and mental agitation caused by overstimulation.

Vrikshasana (*Tree Pose*)

Natarajasana (Dancer Pose):

- Strengthens hip flexors, improves chest expansion for better respiratory function, and increases spinal flexibility.
- Alleviates stiffness from sedentary lifestyles and shallow breathing due to restricted chest muscles.

Natarajasana (*Dancer Pose*)

Virabhadrasana (Warrior Pose):

- Builds leg and hip strength, aligns the spine, and enhances endurance, especially for athletic activities.
- Reduces knee pain caused by weak quadriceps and eases upper back tension from poor posture.

Virabhadrasana (*Warrior Pose*)

Utkatasana (Chair Pose):

- Boosts thigh and glute strength while promoting cardiovascular endurance through sustained muscle engagement.
- Alleviates weak pelvic floor muscles and improves sluggish circulation in the lower body caused by prolonged sitting.

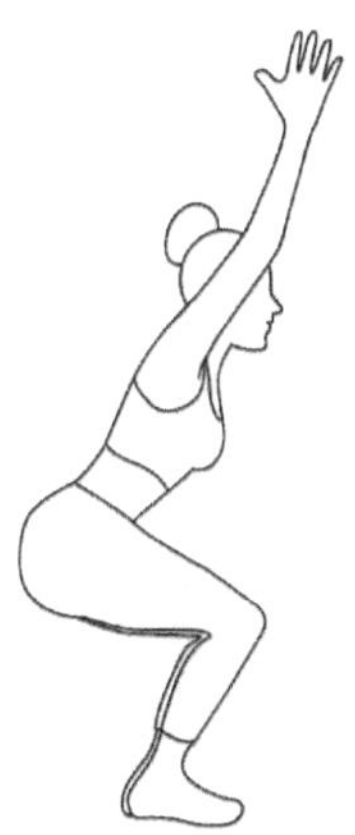

Utkatasana (*Chair Pose*)

Garudasana (Eagle Pose):

- Improves wrist and shoulder mobility, while sharpening focus in distracting environments.

- Relieves shoulder impingement and stiffness resulting from repetitive strain injuries, particularly in the upper body.

Garudasana (*Eagle Pose*)

Seated Series

Gomukhasana (Cow Face Pose):

- Enhances hip, shoulder, and spinal flexibility; supports prostate health (in men) and reproductive health (in women).
- Alleviates shoulder stiffness, lower back discomfort, and emotional stress.

Gomukhasana (*Cow Face Pose*)

Malasana (Garland Pose):

- Improves hip mobility, stimulates digestion, and provides a sense of grounding.
- Relieves stiff hips, supports sluggish metabolism, and enhances focus.

Malasana (*Garland Pose*)

Baddha Konasana (Bound Angle Pose):

- Boosts pelvic circulation, increases inner thigh flexibility, and promotes calmness.
- Eases groin tension, alleviates menstrual discomfort, and reduces anxiety.

Baddha Konasana (*Bound Angle Pose*)

Ardha Matsyendrasana (Half Spinal Twist):

- Improves digestive function, enhances spinal mobility, and promotes energy flow.
- Relieves abdominal bloating, reduces mid-back stiffness, and aids in toxin elimination.

Ardha Matsyendrasana (*Half Spinal Twist*)

Paschim Pranam Asana (Seated Forward Stretch and Bow):

- Strengthens the spine, encourages introspection, and enhances digestive efficiency.
- Alleviates nervous exhaustion, reduces stress, and eases mental fatigue.

Paschim Pranam Asana (*Seated Forward Stretch and Bow*)

On-the-Back Series

Ardha Uttanpadasana (Half Raised-Leg Pose):

- Improves core stability, leg strength, and blood circulation to the lower body.
- Alleviates lower back stiffness, abdominal muscle weakness, and digestive sluggishness.

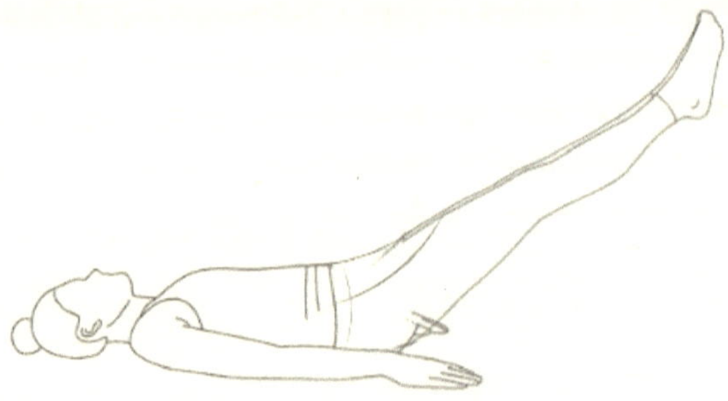

Ardha Uttanpadasana (Half Raised-Leg Pose)

Pavanamuktasana (Wind-Relieving Pose):

- Improves digestive efficiency, abdominal tone, and spinal flexibility.
- Alleviates bloating, gas, constipation, and mild lower back discomfort.

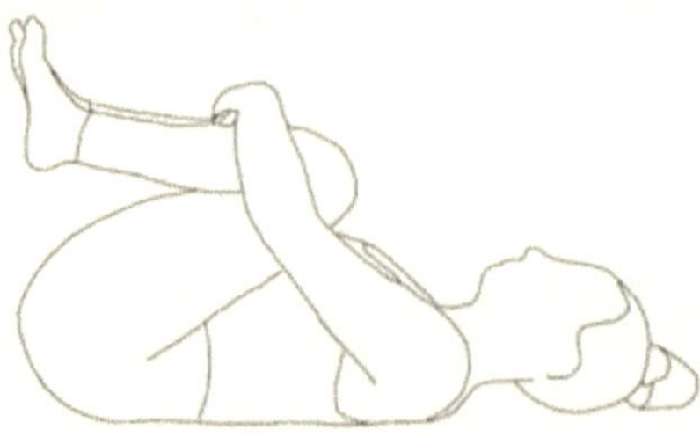

Pavanamuktasana (*Wind Relieving Pose*)

Setu Bandhasana (Bridge Pose):

- Improves spine strength, chest expansion, and energy flow through the body.
- Alleviates back pain, weak glutes, and mild anxiety.

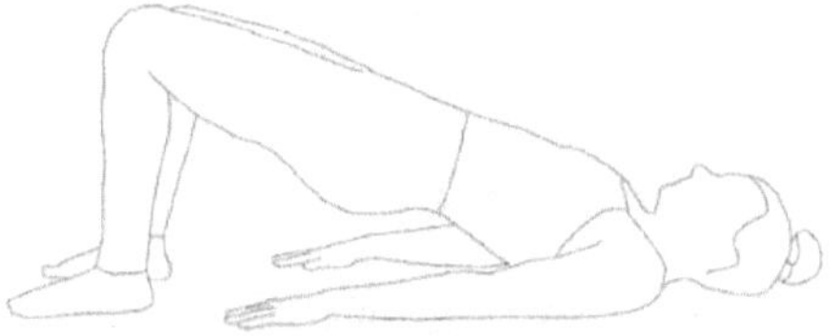

Setu Bandhasana (Bridge Pose)

Supta Baddha Konasana (Reclining Bound Angle Pose):

- Improves pelvic blood circulation, hip flexibility, and relaxation.
- Alleviates stress, menstrual cramps, and fatigue from overexertion.

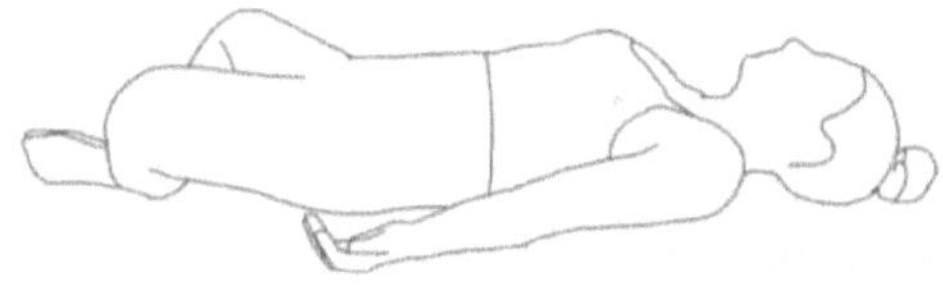

Supta Baddha Konasana (*Reclining Bound Angle Pose*)

Markatasana (Spinal Twist Pose):

- Improves spinal mobility, posture, and digestive flow.
- Alleviates lower back tightness, bloating, and mental stress.

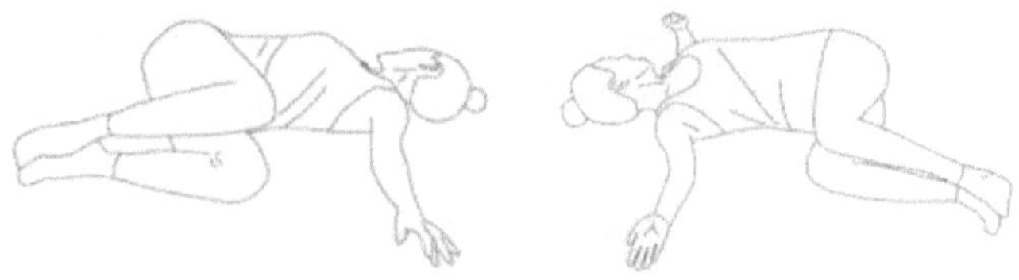

Markatasana (*Spinal Twist Pose*)

On-the-Belly Series

Kumbhakasana (Plank Pose):

- Builds core strength, enhances upper body endurance, and stabilizes the spine.
- Helps mitigate early symptoms of Parkinson's disease, strengthens weak abdominal muscles, and corrects poor posture.

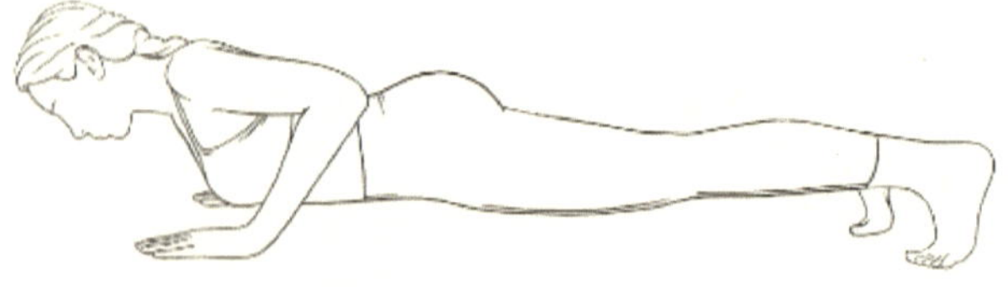

Kumbhakasana (*Plank Pose*)

Bhujangasana (Cobra Pose):

- Enhances spinal flexibility, promotes chest expansion, and increases lung capacity.
- Eases back stiffness, improves respiratory function, and boosts overall circulation.

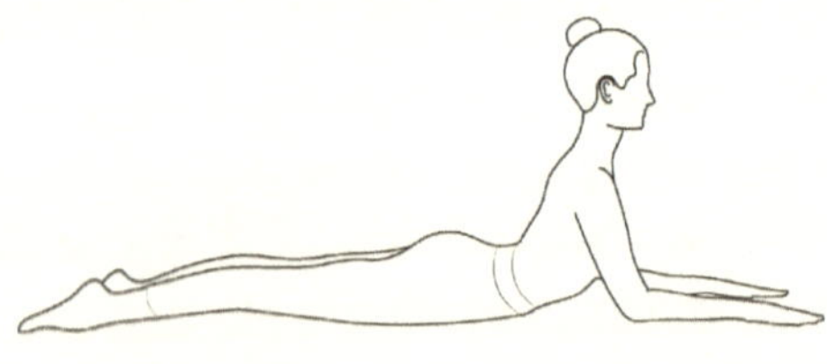

Bhujangasana (*Cobra Pose*)

Dhanurasana (Bow Pose):

- Stimulates digestion, strengthens the back, and improves overall body flexibility.
- Relieves constipation, accelerates a sluggish metabolism, and reduces spinal tension.

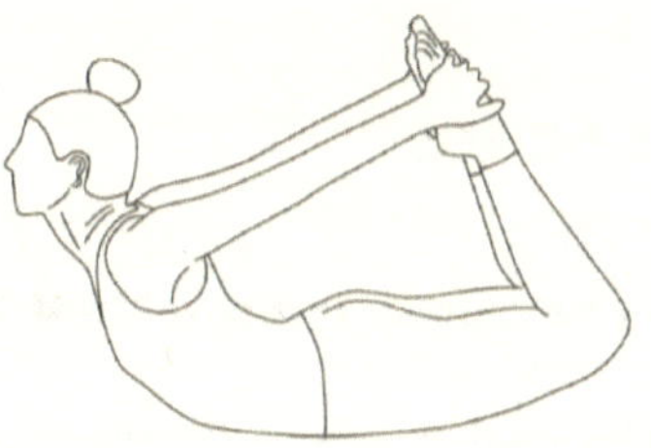

Dhanurasana (*Bow Pose*)

Makarasana (Crocodile Pose):

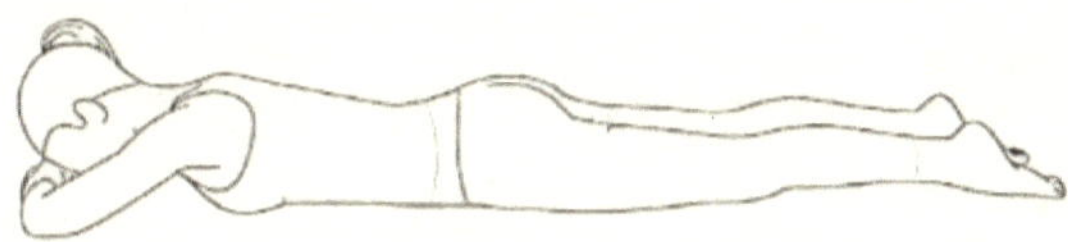

Makarasana (*Crocodile Pose*)

- Encourages deep relaxation, soothes the lower back, and calms the mind.
- Alleviates chronic back pain, reduces anxiety, and combats physical fatigue.

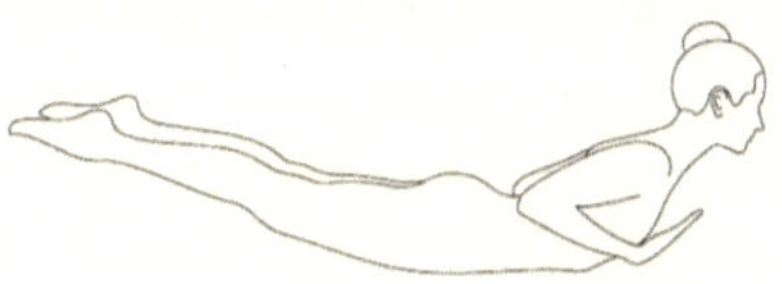

Salabhasana (*Locust Pose*)

Salabhasana (Locust Pose):

- Strengthens the back muscles, corrects posture, and restores energy flow.
- Addresses weak spinal muscles, corrects slouching posture, and improves vitality.

On-the-Knees Series

Supta Vajrasana (Reclined Thunderbolt Pose):

- Enhances flexibility in the thighs and knees, improves spinal posture, and supports digestive health.
- Relieves stiff knees, aids in digestion, and reduces lower back discomfort.

Supta Vajrasana (*Reclined Thunderbolt Pose*)

Simhasana (Lion Pose):

- Promotes throat health, enhances respiratory function, and improves vocal clarity and confidence.
- Eases jaw tension, soothes throat issues, and releases pent-up emotional stress.

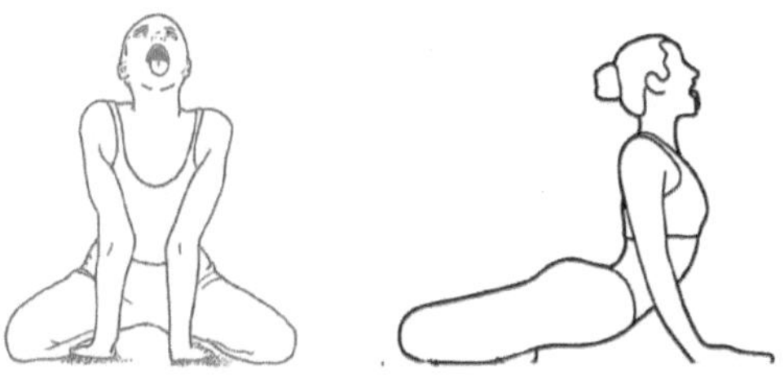

Simhasana (*Lion Pose*)

Marjaryasana-Bitilasana (Cat-Cow Pose): (Figure 23)

- Increases spinal flexibility, improves posture, and boosts overall spinal mobility.
- Alleviates back stiffness, releases muscular tension, and corrects poor spinal posture.

Marjaryasana-Bitilasana (*Cat-Cow Pose*)

Ustrasana (Camel Pose):

- Expands the chest, improves lung capacity, and strengthens the spine.
- Corrects poor posture, alleviates respiratory problems, and helps release emotional blockages.

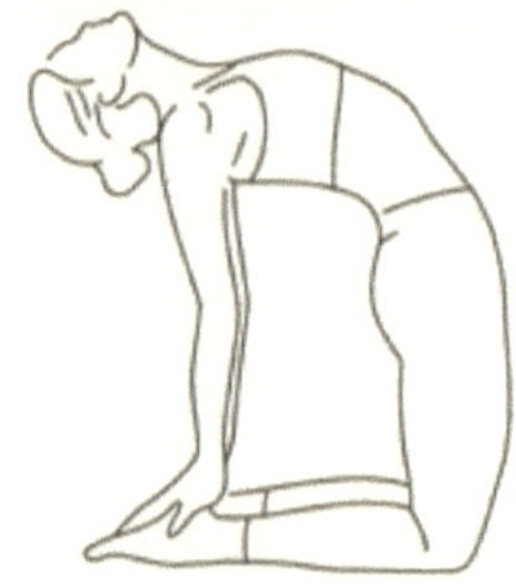

Ustrasana (*Camel Pose*)

Balasana (Child's Pose):

- Encourages deep relaxation, increases lower back flexibility, and enhances mental clarity.
- Reduces stress, alleviates fatigue, and releases tension in the lower back.

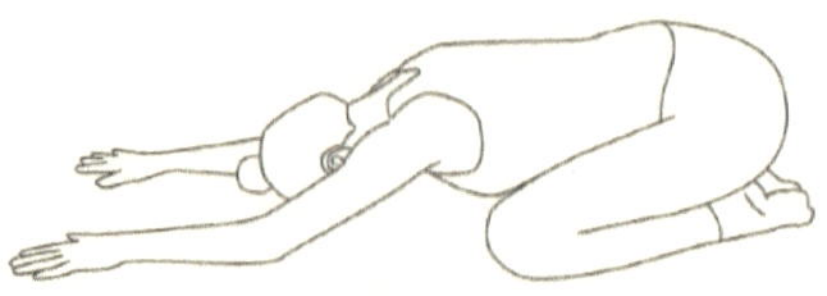

Balasana (*Child's Pose*)

The practice of Asanas is a reminder that growth, whether personal or professional, begins with intention and consistency. Each posture, with its unique benefits, teaches lessons of balance, adaptability, and focus—qualities that resonate deeply in the dynamic world of leadership and business. As you explore these postures, let them serve as anchors, grounding you in the present while preparing you to rise to new heights. The journey through Asanas is not merely about physical mastery but about fostering a state of readiness—an openness to the possibilities within and beyond.

Asanas help transcend the dualities of comfort and discomfort, fostering physical stability, mental focus, and inner balance. They harmonize effort with ease, preparing both the body and mind for deeper practices of Yoga.

Appendix – 6
Balancing the *Panchmahabhootas*: A Yogic Perspective

Ancient yogic philosophy considers that the universe, including the human body, is composed of five fundamental elements: Water (Jal), Fire (Agni), Earth (Prithvi), Air (Vayu), and Space (Akasha). These *Panchmahabhootas* (pronounced 'Punch-maha-bhoota') are the building blocks of life and the cosmos. Yoga aims to balance these elements within us, energizing their latent powers to enhance physical, mental, and spiritual well-being.

Water Element (*Jal*): Fluidity and Adaptability

Water has always held a primal connection for humanity. Submerging in natural water bodies such as rivers, lakes, or oceans is embedded in our genetic memory as a source of profound relaxation and healing. Swimming or immersing oneself in such environments calms the mind, soothes the body, and reawakens an innate connection to nature. Cold water therapy, which has gained prominence in recent days further amplifies these benefits. Brief exposure to cold water boosts circulation, strengthens the immune system, and releases a rush of endorphins, promoting resilience and mental clarity. Whether it is a simple splash of cold water on the face or the intentional practice of ending a shower with revitalizing cold water, this practice invokes the Water element's transformative power, reconnecting us to an ancient yet highly practical ritual.

The Water element symbolizes flow, adaptability, and purification, making it the easiest to invoke among the Panchmahabhootas. It represents the ability to cleanse and refresh, both physically and emotionally. Balancing Water begins with staying hydrated—something as simple yet transformative as drinking warm water in the morning. This ritual jump-starts the body's natural cleansing process, flushing toxins and revitalizing the system. Throughout the day, drinking water at room temperature nourishes the body without shocking it; contrary to popular belief, cold water with ice does little for balance or vitality. Showers, while convenient, often lack the immersive quality needed to connect deeply with this element. A relaxed bath, even once a week, allows for a moment of pause, offering restoration and reconnection with the calming energy of Water.

Physically, the Water element governs the kidneys and bladder—organs responsible for fluid balance and waste filtration. When unbalanced, it can manifest as lower back stiffness, weak knees, or tinnitus. The kidneys' role in bone marrow health links this element to core physical stability. Emotionally, it is tied to intuition and empathy. Like water, emotions are meant to flow freely, cleansing negativity and preventing stagnation. However, imbalance in the Water element can lead to fear, worry, or emotional rigidity.

Fire Element (*Agni*): Energy and Transformation

The Fire element energizes and transforms, symbolizing vitality, enthusiasm, and growth and is slightly more difficult than water to invoke. It fuels digestion and metabolism, converting food into energy and empowering bold actions. On a mental level, Fire fosters clarity, focus, and determination, aligning with moments of peak performance and passion. Activities like brisk walking, jogging, and *Surya Namaskar* (Sun Salutations) naturally invoke this element, sharpening perception and stoking vitality.

The controlled energy of Fire is a double-edged sword. When balanced, it inspires creation, rejuvenation, and the pursuit of meaningful transformations. It empowers us to act decisively and embrace change, but when overactive and ungrounded, this element can lead to burnout, restlessness, and even physical harm. This imbalance is increasingly evident in modern fitness trends, such as High-Intensity Interval Training (HIIT), circuit training, or plyometrics—methods that focus on explosive movements like box jumps, depth jumps, and medicine ball slams to improve power and agility. While these exercises are excellent for invoking the Fire element and enhancing physical fitness, they must be complemented by practices that invoke the other elements. Even if not counterbalanced on the same day, these activities should certainly be incorporated on other days of the week— such as grounding Asanas for Earth, Pranayama for Air, deep relaxation or baths for Water, and meditation for Space.

The Fire element's immense power requires mindful moderation and grounding to prevent it from overwhelming the body and mind. Physiological responses during activities like running or sports—such as increased heart rate, improved circulation, and heightened alertness—reflect Fire's transformative energy. These benefits highlight its potential to spark creativity, resilience, and progress when properly channeled.

Earth Element (*Prithvi*): Stability and Foundation

The Earth element symbolizes grounding, stability, and strength, forming the foundation of our physical existence. Invoked through *Asanas* or isometric exercises like planks, it requires stillness and balance, making it more demanding than Water or Fire. The Earth element encourages physical and mental resilience, creating a profound sense of presence and purpose. Just as the Earth remains steady amidst storms, connecting with this element fosters a calm, centered mind. Grounding exercises not only prevent the overstimulation of

Fire energy but also ensure a harmonious balance, anchoring us to our core values.

This element is deeply connected to the concept of gravitas, often expressed in phrases like "a guy with gravity" or "a personality with weight." Gravitas is the quality of commanding respect, credibility, and a sense of seriousness that gives one's words and actions significance. The Earth element is about cultivating this gravitas—improving not just physical balance but also the balance of character. It is about being grounded in one's truth, speaking with purpose, and carrying oneself with poise and dignity. This inner strength, much like the Earth's unwavering stability, inspires confidence in others.

Through the Earth element, we realize that while motion and progress are important, true strength lies in the stillness and solidity of our foundation. It encourages us to slow down, reflect, and cultivate an inner steadiness that anchors our outward endeavors. By enhancing our gravitas, we strengthen our presence and positively impact our surroundings, radiating stability and assurance that others are naturally drawn to.

Air Element (*Vayu*): Breath and Life Force

The Air element represents freedom, movement, and the flow of life force, or *Prana* and takes even more effort than invoking the Earth element. It is the element most intricately connected to our breath, and the most effective way to invoke and balance it is through *Pranayama*, the ancient practice of breath control. The breath acts as a bridge between the body and the mind, subtly influencing our physical health, mental clarity, and emotional balance. Unlike the Earth or Fire elements, the Air element requires a more deliberate and sustained effort to harmonize, as it invites us to consciously regulate something we often take for granted—our breath. When balanced, it promotes mental agility, emotional freedom, and an expanded sense of awareness that allows us to move beyond our perceived limitations.

The quality of the air we breathe has a profound impact on not just our physical health but also the clarity of our thoughts. In polluted or stale environments, our energy can feel sluggish, and our thinking clouded. One of the simplest ways to improve indoor air quality where most of us spend most of our time is the presence of indoor plants. They not only purify the air but also add an element of natural beauty, restoring a natural balance to sterile spaces and are more impactful than air purifiers. However, *conscious breathing* - slow, mindful inhalations and exhalations, invokes and balances the Air element.

Space Element (*Akasha*): Awareness and Infinity

The Space element is the most challenging to invoke and requires the balance of the other four elements as a foundation. Once activated, it plays a vital role in maintaining harmony among the other elements. Subtle and profound, it symbolizes vastness, intuition, and infinite potential. Space embodies the nothingness that makes everything possible—much like the silence between musical notes that brings depth and meaning to the melody. Pay attention to your favorite music, and you'll notice microseconds of stillness within the sound, a reminder of the power and presence of nothingness. Invoking the Space element requires *Dhyana* or deep meditation and introspection, transcending distractions to access a state of universal consciousness. This state of "mental emptiness" is not about the absence of thought but the presence of boundless awareness, where clarity and creativity flow effortlessly.

Balancing Space means embracing stillness and confronting the vast, infinite depths of the mind. It involves letting go of fears, distractions, and self-imposed boundaries to access the limitless possibilities within. When the Space element is balanced, it fosters an unparalleled sense of connection—both with oneself and the universe—unlocking intuition, wisdom, and the creative force that shapes reality. Through mindfulness and periods of intentional silence, we create the mental expanse needed for true insight and transformation.

The Interplay of the Five Elements

Balancing the *Panchmahabhootas* is not merely a physical practice—it is a profound journey toward achieving harmony and unleashing one's fullest potential. These five elements interact dynamically: Water shapes Earth, Fire purifies Water, Air fuels Fire, and Space holds them all together. Their synergy sustains life, and any imbalance disrupts physical well-being, emotional stability, and spiritual growth.

For successful leadership, balance is not optional—it is essential. Great leaders in business or politics share one common trait: they are profoundly balanced. Their ability to harness the energies of the five elements allows them to lead with clarity, empathy, and impact. By balancing these elements, leaders cultivate resilience, creativity, and adaptability, enabling them to navigate complexity with ease.

Balancing the elements requires deliberate actions and conscious self-care. Water, as the easiest to balance, offers a starting point, while Space, the most subtle, demands deep introspection and finally meditation. Invoking and balancing them creates a state of equilibrium, fostering harmony, purpose, and fulfillment. This balance allows us to live and lead with vitality, joy, and a profound sense of connection to the universe.

Appendix – 7
The Concept of *Drishta* in Yogic Philosophy

In Yogic philosophy, Drishta refers to the "seer" or "witness"—the pure consciousness that observes the mind, body, and external world without attachment or judgment. This concept is integral to understanding the nature of the self and consciousness in various yogic texts and practices.

In Chapter 13 of the Bhagavad Gita, the distinction between the Kshetra (field) and the Kshetragya (knower of the field) is introduced. The Kshetragya, or Drishta, perceives the field of action, comprising the body, mind, and environment, while remaining detached. This detachment allows for wise and compassionate action.

The Yoga Sutras of Patanjali align the concept of Drishta with Purusha (pure consciousness), which observes Prakriti (nature) and its changes without identification. The practice of yoga aims to cultivate this witnessing consciousness, leading to liberation from the fluctuations of the mind.

Practical Application in Modern Contexts

- Mindfulness and Emotional Intelligence: Cultivating the Drishta perspective boosts self-awareness and emotional regulation. Observing as a witness helps individuals handle stress and relationships more effectively.
- Leadership and Decision-Making: Leaders adopting the Drishta mindset make objective decisions and face challenges with clarity, inspiring team confidence.
- Work-Life Integration: Viewing life through Drishta encourages full presence at work and home while maintaining detachment, fostering balance and reducing burnout.

Cultivating the Drishta Perspective

- Meditation: Regular meditation helps strengthen awareness by observing thoughts without attachment.
- Self-Inquiry: Asking "Who am I?" directs attention inward to recognize the self beyond physical and mental identities.
- Mindful Action: Performing tasks with presence and detachment promotes clarity and aligns actions with inner awareness.

The concept of Drishta in yogic philosophy, though seemingly abstract, is a practical tool for self-realization and living. By embodying the observer's role, individuals transcend mental distractions, achieving a balanced and purposeful life. Integrating Drishta into daily habits and leadership turns challenges into opportunities for growth and alignment with one's true nature.

Appendix – 8
The Crypto *Mrigatrishna*

Mrigatrishna (*mree-ga-trish-na*), the Sanskrit word, means the pursuit of something without understanding what is being pursued, a mirage that captivates yet eludes true substance. Crypto, to me, seems like that. Here's why. When I started examining crypto in relation to the Chakras of a business, I found the Root Chakra itself to be missing.

Bitcoin was invented in 2009 by an individual or a group using the pseudonym Satoshi Nakamoto. The lofty vision was a decentralized digital currency, free from government control, not backed by any assets or guarantees from anyone, 'mined' by solving mathematical problems and validated only with transactions through cryptographic algorithms. Bitcoin's creation marked a unique phenomenon in human history: never before had humanity assigned so much material value to something so ethereal.

Let's briefly understand the nuts and bolts of it.

The Problem: Finding the Right "Nonce"

At the core of crypto mining lies a search for a special number, called a nonce (number used once). This number, when combined with specific data from the blockchain, produces a unique output called a hash. The hash is like a lock combination: miners need to find the right nonce to "unlock" the next block in the blockchain.

But here's the twist—the system makes this challenge incredibly difficult. Miners must guess and test millions of potential nonces to find the one that meets the requirements, such as producing a hash with a specific number of leading zeros.

Why Is It So Hard?

This difficulty is intentional. The system adjusts the complexity of the problem to ensure that a new block is mined at a consistent rate (e.g., every 10 minutes for Bitcoin). Think of it as a company that sets increasingly tough key performance indicators (KPIs) for its teams to maintain a steady growth rate, regardless of external circumstances.

Solving these puzzles requires enormous computational power, much like a marathon coding session where developers push their limits to solve complex problems, often leading to mental exhaustion. Miners use specialized computers (mining rigs) to perform these calculations. This process is called Proof of Work (PoW) because miners must prove they have done the work to validate a transaction. Though some newer cryptocurrencies are moving to alternatives like Proof of Stake (PoS), which requires less energy by replacing mining with ownership-based validation, the debate over its scalability and security continues.

Questions That Remain

- Why are these problems necessary beyond securing the blockchain? Could this energy be used for something more productive?
- Who decided the maximum supply of Bitcoin (21 million coins)?
- If Bitcoin is finite, why aren't other cryptocurrencies like Ethereum, Dogecoin, or Litecoin?
- Could advancements like Willow, Google's quantum computing chip, the one that can do in 5 minutes what others would take septillion years to calculate, disrupt this system by solving these problems instantly?
- If something derives its value only by demand and supply, what happens when the supply increases infinitely, in addition to new supply from competitors?

On Tuesday, November 12, 2024, Dogecoin's price surged nearly 20% following Donald Trump's announcement of the "Department of Government Efficiency" (DOGE). Speak of matter over mind! If something derives its value from something as flimsy as this, what happens when one awakens? Or what happens when there is a collective awakening?

What if we, the Business Yoga practitioners, started our own cryptocurrency—Bizcoins and Yogacoins—with a new set of mathematical puzzles for mining? By doing so, would we have created our own Maya: something that exists only because we perceive it to, but in essence, has no real existence?

Appendix – 9
DOSE – Unlocking Happiness

As we have explored throughout *Business Yoga*, the Prana for any business is Customer Experience (CX), which is deeply influenced by Employee Experience (EX). At the heart of employee experience lies employee happiness—a crucial driver of engagement, productivity, and creativity. While the principles of Ashtanga Yoga provide a comprehensive framework for the well-being of businesses, understanding and incorporating structured doses of Dopamine, Oxytocin, Serotonin, and Endorphins (DOSE) can act as a practical guide to fostering happiness in the workplace.

Dopamine: Fostering Achievement and Motivation

Dopamine is the brain's reward chemical, released when we achieve something significant. It inspires action and reinforces positive behavior, making it essential for creating a motivated and goal-driven workforce.

At Kariwala, a simple yet powerful dopamine-boosting practice is the *Happiness Bell*. Every time someone accomplishes something noteworthy, they ring this bell in the presence of their team, celebrating both individual achievement and collective success. This reinforces a culture of recognition and encourages employees to strive for excellence.

Other practices might include regular performance recognition, gamified goal tracking, and milestone celebrations that highlight progress and effort.

Oxytocin: Building Trust and Connection

Oxytocin, often called the "bonding hormone," is vital for fostering trust, collaboration, and emotional safety within teams. A workplace where people feel connected and valued nurtures loyalty and enhances team dynamics.

Leaders can foster oxytocin by promoting empathy and open communication, creating opportunities for team bonding, and encouraging acts of kindness among employees. Simple gestures, such as handwritten thank-you notes or celebrating birthdays, can go a long way in strengthening connections and building a sense of belonging.

Serotonin: Cultivating Confidence and Well-being

Serotonin contributes to feelings of pride, status, and emotional stability. Employees who feel valued and confident are more likely to exhibit high performance and long-term commitment.

Providing opportunities for professional growth, such as training programs or mentorship, can boost serotonin by helping employees feel accomplished and competent. Publicly recognizing team contributions and fostering a culture of mutual respect further reinforces serotonin's positive effects. Additionally, creating a well-lit, vibrant workspace with access to natural light can physically enhance serotonin levels.

Endorphins: Promoting Resilience and Stress Management

Endorphins are natural painkillers that boost resilience and reduce stress. By creating a work environment that balances challenges with moments of joy, businesses can ensure that employees remain engaged and adaptable.

Introducing wellness initiatives, such as yoga or fitness sessions, can stimulate endorphin production. Laughter and humor in the workplace—whether through lighthearted team activities or playful traditions—can also elevate morale and help employees navigate high-pressure situations with ease.

DOSE as a Framework for Business Wellness

While each element of DOSE contributes individually to happiness, their combined effect creates a thriving work environment where employees feel motivated, connected, confident, and resilient. Businesses that consciously integrate DOSE into their culture will find that employee happiness directly enhances customer experience, driving sustainable success.

As you reflect on the lessons of *Business Yoga*, consider DOSE as a practical complement to its principles—a modern, science-backed tool to support the holistic well-being of both your employees and your business. After all, a happy workforce is the foundation of a prosperous organization.

References

Ancient Literature

Rig Veda (ca 5000 BCE or earlier)

Widely regarded as the **oldest book in the world**, the Rig Veda is a collection of hymns dedicated to various deities and forces of nature. Its key themes include the interplay of cosmic order and the importance of harmony between humans and the universe. The Rig Veda highlights unity in diversity and the significance of knowledge and truth as guiding principles.

Upanishads (ca 3500 BCE)

The Upanishads are philosophical treatises forming the conclusion (Vedanta) of the Vedas. A particularly relevant Upanishad for *Business Yoga* is the **Katha Upanishad**, which explores the journey of self-discovery through the story of Nachiketa and Yama, the Lord of Death. Key ideas include the importance of choice, self-mastery, and understanding the eternal truth. These concepts resonate with decision-making, visionary leadership, and harmonizing actions with long-term goals.

Bhagavad Gita (ca 2500 BCE)

A part of the great epic Mahabharata, the Bhagavad Gita is a profound dialogue between Prince Arjuna and Lord Krishna on the battlefield of Kurukshetra. It provides timeless guidance on *Dharma* (duty), *Karma* (action), and *Gyana* (knowledge), emphasizing *Karma Yoga*—selfless action performed without attachment to results. The Gita teaches leaders to connect their actions with a higher purpose, uphold ethical conduct, and develop emotional resilience in the face of challenges.

As a lifelong student of the Gita, it remains my deepest source of inspiration for whatever little I have learned and applied in life. It has also enabled me to connect with fellow reverers—remarkably accomplished individuals from whom I continue to learn through the sheer power of association. Writing *Business Yoga* required resisting the temptation to directly copying and pasting extensive learnings from the Gita, choosing instead to distill its essence into principles applicable to the modern business landscape.

Patanjali Yoga Sutras (ca 200 BCE–400 CE)

This text by Patanjali outlines the philosophy and practice of yoga through the **Ashtanga Yoga (Eightfold Path)**. One of the earliest recorded works on the principles of Yoga, this timeless text encapsulates profound wisdom in just 196 sutras. Handed down orally for millennia before being documented, it remains a cornerstone of Yoga philosophy. Much of the framework for *Business Yoga* is drawn from the Sutras' depth, offering principles that guide clarity, focus, and harmony—essential qualities for leadership and organizational success. Its brevity belies its vast influence, continuing to baffle me, perhaps a few others too and inspire minds across generations. It is divided into four chapters (padas):

1. Samadhi Pada - Focuses on the nature and purpose of yoga.
2. Sadhana Pada - Discusses the practices (including Ashtanga Yoga) needed to progress in yoga.
3. Vibhuti Pada - Explores the powers and abilities that arise from advanced practice.
4. Kaivalya Pada - Describes liberation and the final goal of yoga.

The Arthashastra by Chanakya (Kautilya) (ca 4th Century BCE)

A treatise on statecraft, economics, and military strategy, the Arthashastra by Chanakya offers enduring lessons on leadership, resource management, and diplomacy. It emphasizes strategic thinking, effective governance, and the ethical use of power—principles that remain relevant for optimizing business resources with long-term goals and navigating competitive markets. In school, I naively believed what we were taught—that Adam Smith, with *The Wealth of Nations* in 1776, was the father of economics. It was only much later that I discovered Chanakya's Arthashastra, which predates Smith by nearly 2,000 years.

Zoroastrian Gathas (Hymns of Zoroaster) (ca 1200 BCE)

Attributed to Zoroaster (Zarathustra), the Gathas are hymns that emphasize righteousness, truth (*Asha*), and the worship of Ahura Mazda (the Wise Lord). They advocate ethical leadership, social responsibility, and the pursuit of the greater good. These principles resonate with modern concepts of sustainability and corporate ethics, urging businesses to prioritize values over profit.

I have always been intrigued by the unparalleled respect commanded by the Tata Group in India. Whether it's TCS, the nation's largest software company, the iconic Taj Hotels, the country's largest hotel chain, or industry leaders like Tata Steel, Tata Motors (Jaguar Land Rover), and even Tata Salt, the Tata name consistently symbolizes excellence. Their remarkable diversity—from software to salt—truly speaks volumes! Upon learning about their Zoroastrian roots, I began to wonder if their commitment to Zoroastrian principles of truth, integrity, and service to society has been a driving force behind their extraordinary reputation. It's a fascinating connection that sheds light on their enduring success.

The Dhammapada (ca 3rd Century BCE)

A collection of verses attributed to Buddha, the Dhammapada emphasizes mindfulness, ethical living, and the pursuit of enlightenment. It highlights the importance of compassion, self-control, and mental clarity. These teachings inspire many leaders to build organizations rooted in integrity and empathy, promoting sustainable growth.

The Bible (ca 100 CE)

A collection of religious texts central to Christianity, the Bible offers wisdom on ethical conduct, servant leadership, and the importance of love and compassion. Key ideas, such as the Golden

Rule ("Do unto others as you would have them do unto you"), resonate with principles of fairness and respect in business.

The Yoga Vasistha (ca 10th Century CE)

This philosophical text blends metaphysical stories with practical wisdom. Key themes include the nature of reality, overcoming mental distractions, and achieving liberation through knowledge. Its relevance to business lies in its emphasis on mindfulness, emotional intelligence, and understanding the interconnectedness of actions and outcomes.

Karma Yoga by Swami Vivekananda (1896 CE)

In this modern text, Swami Vivekananda expounds on the concept of *Karma Yoga*—the path of selfless action. He emphasizes doing work as worship, without attachment to the fruits of labor. For businesses, it teaches the value of ethical practices, resilience, and focusing on impact over personal gain, fostering a purpose-driven organizational culture.

Contemporary Literature

Antifragile: *Things That Gain from Disorder* by Nassim Nicholas Taleb

Taleb extends his exploration of uncertainty by introducing antifragility:

- Antifragility Defined: Systems that improve under stress and disorder.

- Optionality: Keep options open to benefit from chaos.
- Skin in the Game: Emphasize accountability and direct stakes in decisions.
- Barbell Strategy: Balance extreme caution with high-risk opportunities.
- The book offers a radical perspective on thriving in volatile environments.

Adiyogi: The Source of Yoga by Sadhguru

This book explores the mythological and historical significance of Adiyogi, the first yogi:

- Adiyogi's Teachings: Foundations of yoga as a science for self-realization.
- Universal Wisdom: Insights that transcend cultural and temporal boundaries.
- Yoga as a Science: Emphasizes yoga's role in unlocking human potential.
- Myth and Reality: Combines storytelling with philosophical depth.
- A profound exploration of yoga's origins and its relevance to modern seekers.

Atomic Habits: An Easy & Proven Way to Build Good Habits & Break Bad ones by James Clear

Clear provides a framework for transforming behaviors to achieve lasting change:

- The Habit Loop: Master the process of cue, craving, response, and reward to build habits that stick.
- Four Laws of Behavior Change: Develop positive habits by making them obvious, attractive, easy, and satisfying.
- Small Changes, Big Results: Demonstrates how incremental improvements lead to profound transformations.

- Identity-Based Habits: Shift focus from outcomes to the type of person you aspire to be.

A practical guide to achieving remarkable results by focusing on systems rather than goals

---

Beyond Three Generations: *The Definitive Guide to Building Enduring Indian Family Businesses by Firoz Meeran, MSA Kumar, George Skaria and Navas Meeran*

This book explores the challenges and opportunities of Indian family businesses aiming for longevity. It provides actionable insights for:

- Generational Transition: Ensuring smooth leadership handovers while maintaining family harmony.
- Governance Structures: Implementing formal mechanisms for effective management and conflict resolution.
- Values and Vision: Integrating core family values with a sustainable business vision.
- Adaptation and Innovation: Staying relevant through evolving markets without losing foundational principles.

The book includes real-life examples, offering strategies to balance tradition with modern business demands, ensuring success across generations

---

Crucial Conversations: *Tools for Talking When Stakes Are High* by Joseph Grenny

Grenny provides tools for navigating difficult but essential conversations:

- Mastering Dialogue: Prioritize open, respectful communication over monologues.
- Safety First: Create an environment where all parties feel safe to express themselves.

- Overcoming Silence or Violence: Avoid shutting down or reacting aggressively.
- Actionable Steps: Move conversations toward clear agreements and commitments.
- The book equips readers with skills for resolving conflicts and building stronger relationships.

Compassionate Leadership: *How to Do Hard Things in a Human Way* by Rasmus Hougaard and Jacqueline Carter

This book highlights the importance of leading with empathy while maintaining effectiveness:

- Balancing Compassion and Strength: Combine empathy with wisdom to navigate challenges.
- Human-Centered Leadership: Prioritize employee well-being and growth.
- Difficult Conversations: Handle sensitive topics with care and understanding.
- Team Building: Foster collaboration and trust to enhance performance.
- This book provides practical tools for leaders to manage with both heart and results.

Chakra Healing for Beginners: *A Practical Guide to Balancing Energy Centers for Personal and Professional Success* by Callie Parker

Palmer's book explores the alignment of the seven chakras with different aspects of business, emphasizing how energy imbalances can manifest as challenges in communication, leadership, or financial stability.

Key ideas:

- Root Chakra: Foundations like structure and profitability.
- Sacral Chakra: Creativity and vision in innovation.

- Heart Chakra: Emotional connections and relationships with clients and teams.

By balancing these energy centers, the book provides strategies for personal reflection and business growth, fostering healthier, more successful organizations.

Creative Confidence: *Unleashing the Creative Potential Within Us All* by Tom Kelley and David Kelley

A practical guide to unlocking creativity and fostering innovation, the book underscores that creativity is a skill anyone can develop. Key insights include:

- Creativity as a Learnable Skill: Creativity is nurtured through practice and experimentation.
- Embrace Failure: Failure is a stepping stone to success, offering valuable lessons.
- The Power of Play: Playfulness sparks innovative ideas and unconventional solutions.
- Collaboration: Diverse perspectives enhance problem-solving and creativity.
- Overcoming Creative Blocks: Shift environments, take breaks, or change approaches to reignite creativity.
- This book encourages readers to embrace their creative potential, transforming challenges into opportunities.

Drive: *The Surprising Truth About What Motivates Us* by Daniel H. Pink

Pink explores motivation through the lens of human psychology:

- Intrinsic Motivation: Highlights the importance of autonomy, mastery, and purpose.
- Carrot-and-Stick Limitations: Challenges traditional reward-punishment systems.

- The Power of Purpose: Connects meaningful work with sustained motivation.
- Practical Applications: Provides strategies for creating motivation-friendly environments.

The book reframes motivation as an internal drive rather than external incentives.

Deep Work: *Rules for Focused Success in a Distracted World* by Cal Newport

Newport argues that the ability to engage in focused, uninterrupted work is a critical skill in the modern world:

- Deep Work vs. Shallow Work: Prioritize meaningful, high-value tasks over low-effort distractions.
- Time Blocking: Schedule specific periods for focused work.
- Digital Minimalism: Reduce distractions from social media and notifications.
- Deliberate Practice: Continuously improve by pushing cognitive limits.
- The book serves as a guide to cultivating focus and achieving professional excellence.

Emotional Intelligence: *Why It Can Matter More Than IQ* by Daniel Goleman Goleman outlines five components of emotional intelligence:

- Self-Awareness: Understanding your emotions.
- Self-Regulation: Controlling impulses and adapting to change.
- Motivation: Staying driven by inner values and goals.
- Empathy: Recognizing others' emotions and perspectives.
- Social Skills: Building relationships and managing teams effectively. The key takeaway is that emotional intelligence,

more than IQ, drives success in leadership and personal effectiveness.

Energy Leadership: *The 7-Level Framework for Mastery in Life and Business* by Bruce D. Schneider

Schneider explores how energy levels influence personal and organizational success:

- Energy Awareness: Recognize how attitudes and emotions impact performance.
- Seven Levels of Energy: Shift from catabolic (draining) to anabolic (constructive) energy.
- Leadership Impact: Empower teams by managing energy effectively.
- Practical Application: Use the framework to enhance productivity and relationships.
- This book equips readers with tools to elevate energy and drive success.

Enlightenment Now: *The Case for Reason, Science, Humanism, and Progress* by Steven Pinker

Pinker champions the achievements of the Enlightenment, highlighting humanity's progress through reason, science, and humanism:

- Data-Driven Progress: Evidence of advancements in health, wealth, safety, and education.
- Humanism's Role: Advocates moral progress through empathy and universal rights.
- Reason as a Tool: Emphasizes the importance of critical thinking and evidence-based decision-making.
- Optimism Revisited: Challenges pessimism with a realistic yet hopeful outlook.

The book inspires readers to see progress as a path forward, fueled by Enlightenment ideals.

Enlightened Capitalists: *Cautionary Tales of Business Pioneers Who Tried to Do Well by Doing Good* by James O'Toole

O'Toole explores how business leaders can combine profitability with social responsibility:

- Ethical Leadership: Focus on moral practices alongside financial success.
- Purpose Beyond Profit: Emphasizes societal and environmental contributions.
- Sustainability: Highlights long-term benefits of ethical business models.
- Challenges and Trade-offs: Explores the difficulties of balancing profit and purpose.

The book provides a nuanced view of how businesses can act as a force for good while staying competitive.

Emotion and Relationships: *Bond or Bondage* by Sadhguru

Sadhguru emphasizes mindfulness and presence as keys to a fulfilling life:

- The Power of Now: Focus on living fully in the present moment.
- Detachment: Letting go of past regrets and future anxieties.
- Mindfulness Practices: Tools for cultivating awareness and gratitude.
- Inner Liberation: How presence leads to freedom from suffering.
- A practical and philosophical guide to embracing the present for a richer life experience.

Eternal Echoes: *A Book of Poems* by Sadhguru

This book explores themes of connection and timeless wisdom:

- Interconnectedness: Understanding the unity between self and the cosmos.
- Ancient Wisdom: Reflections on spirituality's enduring relevance.
- Life and Death: Contemplates the cycles of existence and renewal.
- Universal Truths: Insights that inspire a deeper understanding of life.
- A reflective work that bridges ancient philosophy with modern understanding.

Forgiveness: *A Bold Choice for a Peaceful Heart* by Dr. Robin Casarjian

This book explores Forgiveness as a conscious choice for personal healing. Casarjian challenges common misconceptions, emphasizing that forgiveness is not about condoning harm but about releasing oneself from resentment. Key takeaways include:

- Redefining Forgiveness: Forgiveness as a personal choice for healing, not requiring reconciliation.
- Addressing Misconceptions: Debunking myths about diminishing the offense.
- Highlighting Benefits: Emphasizing improved health, well-being, and stronger relationships.
- Practical Approach: Outlining a practical approach to releasing resentment.

Through real-life stories, Casarjian provides tools to navigate the complexities of forgiveness and discover inner peace.

Grit: *The Power of Passion and Perseverance* by Angela Duckworth

Duckworth emphasizes grit—sustained passion and effort—as a key to success:

- Grit vs. Talent: Perseverance outweighs natural talent in achieving goals.
- Growth Mindset: Believe in the potential for improvement through effort.
- Practical Strategies: Set clear goals, practice deliberately, and embrace challenges.
- Duckworth's insights inspire individuals to cultivate resilience and long-term focus.

Give and Take: *A Revolutionary Approach To Success* by Adam Grant

Grant explores how generosity can drive success in life and business:

- Givers vs. Takers: Givers prioritize helping others, while takers focus on self-interest.
- Reciprocity: Effective givers balance generosity with boundaries to avoid burnout.
- Networking and Collaboration: Helping others creates long-term success and loyalty.
- Grant argues that cultivating a giving mindset leads to deeper connections and sustainable success.

Heal The Chakras Of Your Business: *Adapt Ancient Wellness Systems For The Wealth Of Your Business Today* by Lynn M. Scheurell

Scheurell adapts the Ayurvedic chakra system to business growth and success.

- Business Energy Centers: Balance aspects like vision, communication, and relationships with chakra energy.

- Strategic Questions: Provides diagnostic tools for identifying imbalances in business energy flow.
- Growth Through Awareness: Focuses on personal development as a driver for organizational success.
- Holistic Framework: Combines metaphysical concepts with actionable business strategies.

Hands of Light: *A Guide to Healing Through the Human Energy Field* by Barbara Ann Brennan

This visually engaging book offers a clear introduction to chakras.

- History and Symbolism: Traces the origins and meanings of the chakra system.
- Illustrated Insights: Combines imagery with concise explanations for better understanding.
- Practical Tips: Provides simple techniques for balancing and maintaining energy flow.

Inner Engineering: *A Yogi's Guide to Joy* by Sadhguru

Sadhguru introduces tools for inner transformation:

- Inner Awareness: Unite thoughts, emotions, and actions.
- Practical Wisdom: Simple practices for improving focus, health, and relationships.
- Self-Mastery: Cultivate joy by managing inner energies effectively.
- This book bridges ancient yogic principles with modern life challenges.

Karma: *A Yogi's Guide to Crafting Your Destiny* by Sadhguru

Sadhguru redefines the concept of karma, emphasizing conscious action:

- Karma as Action, Not Fate: Your actions shape your experience, not external forces.

- Freedom Through Awareness: Break habitual patterns by acting with mindfulness.
- Adhere to Dharma: Live in harmony with your purpose for fulfillment.
- The book offers tools for transcending past influences and crafting a meaningful life.

Letting Go: *The Pathway of Surrender* by David R. Hawkins

Hawkins introduces surrender as a tool for personal growth and spiritual liberation:

- Surrender Defined: Releasing attachments and resistance to find peace.
- Practical Techniques: Methods for letting go of negative emotions and patterns.
- Inner Freedom: Liberation through acceptance and presence in the moment.
- Growth through Surrender: Living authentically by releasing fears and expectations.
- A transformative book for those seeking peace and self-realization.

Leadership That Gets Results by Daniel Goleman

Goleman identifies six leadership styles rooted in emotional intelligence:

- Coercive: Drives compliance but stifles creativity.
- Authoritative: Mobilizes teams toward a compelling vision.
- Affiliative: Builds emotional bonds and harmony.
- Democratic: Encourages participation and consensus.
- Pacesetting: Sets high standards but risks burnout.
- Coaching: Develops individuals for long-term growth.
- The key takeaway is flexibility: effective leaders adapt their style to suit the context and team dynamics.

My Life in Full: Work, Family, and Our Future by Indra Nooyi

Nooyi chronicles her journey from her upbringing in India to becoming PepsiCo's CEO:

- Balancing Work and Family: Insights into managing a demanding career and personal responsibilities.
- Leadership Lessons: Nooyi shares strategies for leading with purpose and resilience.
- Future of Work: Advocates for diversity, sustainability, and inclusive leadership.
- This memoir provides inspiration and practical lessons for navigating professional and personal challenges.

Restoring the Soul of Business: Staying Human in the Age of Data by **Rishad Tobaccowala**

This book redefines the role of employees in the modern workplace:

- Human-Centric Leadership: Emphasizes individuality and creativity.
- Emotional Intelligence: Leverages empathy and connection in leadership.
- Purpose-Driven Culture: Bridges employees' values with organizational goals.
- Innovation Through Humanity: Unlocks potential by treating employees as collaborators.
- An inspiring call to value people as integral partners in business success.

Relational Intelligence: The People Skills You Need For The Life Of Purpose You Want by Dr. Dharius Daniels

This book explores the concept of *Relational Intelligence*, the ability to discern and manage relationships effectively. Daniels emphasizes that success and fulfillment are deeply influenced by the quality of our connections. Key takeaways include:

- Four Types of Relationships: The book categorizes relationships into friends, associates, assignments, and advisors, helping readers assess and prioritize their connections.
- Boundary Setting: Emphasizes the importance of establishing boundaries to protect emotional and mental well-being.
- Purposeful Relationships: Encourages fostering connections that reverb with personal values and life goals.
- Relational Growth: Highlights the need to continually evaluate and adapt relationships as we evolve personally and professionally.

Through practical advice and engaging storytelling, Daniels provides tools to help readers build and sustain meaningful, impactful relationships that enrich both their personal and professional lives.

Start with Why: *How Great Leaders Inspire Everyone to Take Action* by Simon Sinek

Sinek argues that great leaders and organizations inspire by starting with "Why":

- The Golden Circle: Success stems from clarity in purpose (Why), process (How), and product (What).
- Purpose-Driven Leadership: Align actions with a core mission to inspire loyalty and innovation.
- Emotional Connection: Foster trust and engagement by emphasizing values and beliefs.
- Sinek's principles encourage leaders to lead with vision and authenticity.

Secrets of The Divine Business Code by Kelly Vikings

This book inspires business leaders to connect with their authentic selves while navigating modern challenges.

- Divine Harmony: Encourages leaders to integrate business strategies with personal values and purpose.
- Empowerment Tools: Offers exercises for boosting confidence, clarity, and intuition in leadership.
- Growth Mindset: Focuses on nurturing success through authenticity and self-awareness.
- Practical Resources: Includes access to a free workbook for actionable exercises and strategies.

Transcendence: *My Spiritual Experiences with Pramukh Swamiji* by Dr. APJ Abdul Kalam

Dr. Kalam shares his spiritual journey with Pramukh Swamiji:

- Spiritual Guidance: The role of Pramukh Swamiji's teachings in shaping Dr. Kalam's spiritual and personal growth.
- Selflessness and Service: Emphasis on humility and selfless service as a path to true fulfillment.
- Faith and Purpose: How spirituality provides clarity, purpose, and resilience in life.
- Integrating Science and Spirituality: The harmonious balance between intellectual pursuits and spiritual wisdom.

The Work-Life Balance Myth: *Rethinking Your Optimal Balance for Success* by David J. McNeff

This book challenges traditional notions of work-life balance by introducing the "Seven Slices of Life" framework:

- Career: Achieving professional success without compromising other aspects of life.

- Family: Prioritizing meaningful relationships.
- Health: Maintaining physical and mental well-being.
- Friends: Cultivating supportive social connections.
- Hobbies: Pursuing personal interests for fulfillment.
- Spirituality: Finding purpose and inner peace.

Community: Engaging with the broader world to create impact.

A practical guide to creating harmony and fulfillment across life's interconnected facets.

The Power of Full Engagement: *Managing Energy, Not Time, Is the Key to High Performance and Personal Renewal* by Jim Loehr and Tony Schwartz

The authors argue that managing energy, not time, is key to peak performance:

- Energy Management: Focus on physical, emotional, mental, and spiritual energy.
- Balance and Recovery: Avoid burnout by alternating stress with renewal.
- Positive Routines: Develop habits that maximize energy and focus.
- Purpose-Driven Work: Unite actions with personal values and goals.
- A blueprint for achieving sustainable high performance and personal renewal.

The Minimalist Home: *A Room-by-Room Guide to a Decluttered, Refocused Life* by Joshua Becker

Becker advocates for decluttering to create a more intentional and fulfilling life:

- Decluttering for Clarity: Simplify living spaces to reduce stress.

- Focus on Essentials: Prioritize only what truly adds value to life.
- Intentional Living: Redirect time and energy toward meaningful pursuits.
- Well-Being: Improved mental and emotional health through minimalism.
- A practical guide to achieving a more focused, peaceful, and fulfilling life.

The Almanack of Naval Ravikant: *A Guide to Wealth and Happiness* by Eric Jorgensen

A compilation of Naval Ravikant's insights on wealth and happiness:

- Wealth Creation: Advocates leveraging knowledge, tools, and networks.
- Happiness Framework: Focus on mindfulness, self-awareness, and detachment.
- Decision-Making: Emphasizes rational thinking and long-term strategies.
- Compounding Benefits: Highlights the power of time and continuous learning.

The book serves as a guide for achieving success and fulfillment in life and work.

Transcendence: *The New Science of Self-Actualization* by Scott Barry Kaufman

Kaufman revisits Maslow's hierarchy of needs with modern psychological insights:

- Self-Actualization Revisited: Focus on human growth beyond basic needs.

- Integration of Science and Philosophy: Blends traditional wisdom with contemporary research.
- Transcendence Defined: Achieving fulfillment by connecting with something greater than oneself.
- Practical Steps: Offers guidance for cultivating creativity, purpose, and well-being.

The book modernizes Maslow's concepts, making them relevant to personal and professional growth.

The Yoga and Chakras of Business: *Streamlining Businesses and Organizations through Yoga and Chakras Knowledge* by Germán Puentes

Puentes applies the principles of yoga and chakras to business management and organizational health.

- Chakra Mapping for Businesses: Synchronize chakras with leadership, operations, and strategy.
- Diagnostic Tools: Techniques to assess and improve energy flow in an organization.
- Practical Applications: Suggests team-building exercises and restructuring methods to balance business energy.

The Art of War: *Spirituality For Conflict* by Sun Tzu

This ancient text outlines timeless strategies for achieving victory with minimal conflict:

- Know Yourself and the Enemy: Success requires understanding strengths, weaknesses, and intentions.
- Deception and Timing: Surprise and strategic patience are key to gaining the upper hand.
- Avoid Unnecessary Battles: True mastery lies in winning without fighting.
- Sun Tzu's principles remain relevant for leadership and competitive strategy.

Transcendence: *Healing And Transformation Through Transcendental Meditation* by Norman E. Rosenthal

Rosenthal explores the impact of Transcendental Meditation (TM) on mental and physical well-being:

- Stress Reduction: TM significantly lowers stress and anxiety.
- Enhanced Creativity: Regular practice promotes clarity and innovative thinking.
- Improved Health: TM positively impacts cardiovascular and neurological health.
- This book offers scientific and anecdotal evidence for incorporating mindfulness into daily life.

The Speed of Trust: *The One Thing That Changes Everything* by Stephen M.R. Covey

Covey emphasizes the critical role of trust in personal and professional success:

- Foundation of Trust: Trust accelerates decision-making and enhances relationships.
- Five Waves of Trust: Build trust through integrity, intent, capabilities, results, and relationships.
- Cost of Distrust: Lack of trust leads to inefficiency, higher costs, and damaged relationships.
- Covey outlines actionable steps to build and maintain trust within teams and organizations.

The Innovator's Dilemma: *When New Technologies Cause Great Firms to Fail* by Clayton Christensen

Christensen explores why successful companies often fail to adopt disruptive innovations:

- Disruptive Innovation: Emerging technologies disrupt established markets by targeting niche or low-end users.

- Sustaining vs. Disruptive Technologies: Companies often focus on improving existing products rather than exploring groundbreaking innovations.
- Market Adaptation: Businesses must adapt their strategies to embrace innovation and changing consumer demands.
- Christensen's insights serve as a blueprint for staying relevant in rapidly evolving industries.

The Architecture of Happiness by Alain de Botton

De Botton explores the profound impact of architecture on human emotions and well-being:

- Psychology of Space: The design of buildings influences moods and behavior.
- Community Building: Thoughtful architecture fosters social interaction and belonging.
- Aesthetic Importance: Beauty in architecture enhances quality of life.
- Daily Impact: Well-designed homes, workplaces, and public spaces elevate productivity and happiness.
- This book invites readers to consider the emotional and psychological effects of their built environments.

The Black Swan: *The Impact of the Highly Improbable* by Nassim Nicholas Taleb

Taleb explores the impact of rare, high-impact events and their unpredictability:

- Black Swan Events: Unpredictable events with massive consequences.
- Fragility vs. Antifragility: Systems must not only withstand shocks but benefit from them.
- Narrative Fallacy: Avoid oversimplified stories to explain complex phenomena.

- Embrace Uncertainty: Focus on resilience and optionality to handle the unexpected.
- Taleb challenges conventional risk management, advocating for embracing randomness as a strength.

The Goal: *A Process of Ongoing Improvement* by Eliyahu M. Goldratt

Goldratt introduces the Theory of Constraints (TOC), a systematic approach to improving business processes:

- Identify the Constraint: Determine the bottleneck limiting performance.
- Exploit the Constraint: Maximize the output of the limiting factor.
- Subordinate Other Processes: Adjust other activities to support the constraint.
- Elevate the Constraint: Invest resources to reduce the constraint's impact.
- Continuous Improvement: Reassess and address new constraints as they arise.
- The book underscores that solving the most critical bottleneck leads to significant, sustainable improvements.

The E-Myth Revisited: *Why Most Small Businesses Don't Work and What to Do About It* by Michael E. Gerber

Gerber debunks the myth that technical expertise alone guarantees entrepreneurial success:

- Three Roles: Successful business owners balance being Entrepreneurs, Managers, and Technicians.
- Systems Thinking: Build scalable businesses by implementing replicable systems and processes.
- Avoid Premature Scaling: Establish strong foundations before expanding operations.

- This book provides a roadmap for turning small businesses into sustainable enterprises.

The Art of Innovation: *Lessons in Creativity* by Tom Kelley

Kelley demystifies the creative process, emphasizing practical strategies for fostering innovation in organizations:

- Human-Centered Design: Understand and prioritize user needs for impactful solutions.
- Prototyping: Build quick prototypes to refine ideas iteratively.
- Collaborative Teams: Diverse teams enhance problem-solving and innovation.
- Curiosity-Driven Leadership: Encourage curiosity and openness to fuel creativity.
- Kelley demonstrates how innovation emerges from empathy, experimentation, and collaboration.

The 7 Habits of Highly Effective People by Stephen R. Covey

Covey's timeless classic presents a holistic framework for personal and professional success, outlined in seven transformative habits:

- Be Proactive: Take responsibility for actions and focus on controllable factors.
- Begin with the End in Mind: Define clear goals guided by a personal mission.
- Put First Things First: Prioritize the important over urgent tasks for long-term results.
- Think Win-Win: Foster mutually beneficial relationships and adopt an abundance mindset.
- Seek First to Understand, Then to Be Understood: Practice empathetic listening before expressing opinions.

- Synergize: Collaborate to achieve greater outcomes through teamwork and diversity.
- Sharpen the Saw: Invest in physical, mental, social, and spiritual renewal for sustained effectiveness.
- By mastering these habits, readers can sync their actions with their values, fostering growth and fulfillment.

Off Balance: *Getting Beyond the Work-Life Balance Myth to Personal and Professional Satisfaction* by Matthew Kelly

This book critiques the pursuit of work-life balance and advocates for meaningful harmony:

- Satisfaction Over Balance: Focus on living a values-driven life.
- Strategic Imbalance: Embrace life's natural shifts with purpose.
- Personal Fulfillment: Balance actions with core beliefs and aspirations.
- Professional Growth: Foster success while staying true to personal goals.
- A transformative guide to designing a life of authenticity and fulfillment.

Vastu Living: *Creating A Home For The Soul* by **Kathleen Cox**

This book explores Vastu, the Indian practice of designing spaces to enhance health and harmony:

- Vastu Principles: How space arrangement influences energy flow, health, and prosperity.
- Healing Spaces: Transforming environments to support mental and spiritual wellness.
- Practical Tips: Easy ways to apply Vastu in modern homes and workplaces.

- Cox's guide offers both an introduction to Vastu and practical advice for creating balanced, energy-enhancing spaces.

What Got You Here Won't Get You There: *How Successful People Become Even More Successful* by Marshall Goldsmith

Goldsmith challenges leaders to evolve beyond their past success:

- Success Barriers: Recognize behaviors that hinder further growth.
- Self-Awareness: Identify and address habits that limit effectiveness.
- Feedback and Change: Embrace feedback to refine leadership skills.
- Building Relationships: Develop stronger connections for sustained success.
- A practical guide for leaders to overcome complacency and achieve continued growth.

Wheels of Life: *The Classic Guide To The Chakra System* by Anodea Judith

Judith's book provides an in-depth exploration of the chakras, their attributes, and their influence on physical, emotional, and spiritual health.

- Chakra Framework: Explains each chakra's qualities, symbolism, and significance.
- Holistic Health: Discusses how imbalances manifest in health and how to address them.
- Practical Guidance: Includes meditations, visualizations, and techniques for chakra balancing.

*7 **Chakras of Management:** Wisdom from Indic Scriptures by Ashutosh Garg*

This book combines management theory with ancient Indian philosophy, exploring the chakras as energy centers for effective leadership and organizational success. Key insights include:

- Emotional Intelligence: The heart chakra fosters empathy, compassion, and emotional balance, essential for leadership.
- Effective Communication: The throat chakra enhances clarity and articulation, enabling leaders to inspire and engage their teams.
- Rational Decision-Making: The mind chakra supports intellectual clarity and strategic thinking.
- Relationship Building: The solar plexus chakra reinforces self-esteem and trust, crucial for teamwork.
- Purpose-Driven Leadership: The crown chakra connects to spirituality and vision, guiding leaders toward meaningful goals.

The book offers practical exercises to balance and activate chakras, presenting a unique blend of ancient wisdom and modern management strategies for effective leadership.

About the Author

Anil Kariwala is a globally recognized entrepreneur and UN Awardee for Women Empowerment, leading a team of over 1,000 joyful individuals with three decades of business experience. His mission-driven organization, Kariwala Industries Ltd., manufactures uniforms and sustainable bags, exemplifying ethical practices, sustainability, and profitability, guided by the philosophy of "spreading happiness through business with principles of Dharma." 

Anil is an accountant three times over by qualification—holding CA, CMA, and CPA designations—and is a lifelong student committed to continuous learning. His executive education includes the latest from the Stanford Seed Transformation Program at Stanford GSB. Always in a state of joy, Anil defies what most would call a busy business schedule by dedicating time to teaching youngsters, mentoring upcoming entrepreneurs, and pursuing his creative passions. He has recorded 11 music albums, available on Spotify, Apple Music, iTunes, Amazon Music, and YouTube, and has held five fully sold-out concerts to raise funds for various charitable organizations.

Anil is a teacher at heart, and nothing satisfies him more than the "wow moments" of someone who has learned something from him. He also served for six years as a pivotal board member of London-based Sedex, the world's largest organization enabling responsible supply chains. With cross-cultural insights gained from traveling to over 40 countries, Anil brings a unique perspective on building joyful, sustainable leadership in today's global business environment.

Author's LinkedIn Profile   Business Yoga Forum

Index

www.ingramcontent.com/pod-product-compliance
Lightning Source LLC
Chambersburg PA
CBHW032004150726
47990CB00005B/1827